Repairing Anxious and Avoidant Attachment Styles

Recover Insecure Relationships, Rewire Emotional Patterns, and Build Lasting Connections with Attachment Theory Tools That Work

Kaelen Dovewell

Copyright © 2025 by Kaelen Dovewell
All rights reserved.

No part of this publication may be reproduced, distributed, or transmitted in any form or by any means, including photocopying, recording, or other electronic or mechanical methods, without the prior written permission of the publisher, except in the case of brief quotations used in critical reviews or scholarly discussions.

This book is a work of informational and emotional support. It is not intended as a substitute for professional psychological, psychiatric, or medical advice, diagnosis, or treatment. If you are in need of mental health support, please consult with a qualified healthcare provider.

Table of Contents

Preface 7
Introduction: A New Path to Emotional Security 15
    The Problem with Traditional Relationship Advice 15
    What Emotional Security Actually Feels Like ... 17
    The Promise of the Work Ahead 18
    A Different Kind of Love Story 20
PART I: UNDERSTANDING ATTACHMENT — THE ROOT OF RELATIONSHIP STRUGGLES 22
    Chapter 1: What Is Attachment Theory, Really? 23
        The Science Behind Early Bonds 23
        The Four Major Attachment Styles Explained .. 25
        Why Understanding This Changes Everything. 29
    Chapter 2: Anxious Attachment — The Fear of Abandonment 32
        Origins in Childhood Dynamics 32
        Common Behaviors in Adult Relationships 34
        Emotional Triggers and Reinforcement Loops .. 37
    Chapter 3: Avoidant Attachment — The Fear of Intimacy 41
        Disconnection as a Coping Mechanism 41
        Emotional Suppression and Self-Sufficiency 43
        How Avoidance Shapes Romantic and Social Bonds 46
PART II: THE COST OF INSECURE ATTACHMENT IN ADULT LIFE 50
    Chapter 4: The Push-Pull Dance in Relationships .. 51
        Why Anxious and Avoidant Partners Often Attract 51

Co-dependency, Distancing, and Misattunement. 53

Real-Life Case Study: Breaking the Cycle........57

Chapter 5: Emotional Dysregulation and Unhealed Patterns.. 60

How Attachment Wounds Disrupt Emotional Flow... 60

Recognizing Your Emotional Survival Strategies.. 62

The Nervous System's Role in Reactivity..........65

Chapter 6: Self-Sabotage and Fear of Vulnerability... 68

Walls Built by Avoidance, Cravings of the Anxious... 68

How Fear Manifests as Control, Withdrawal, or Clinginess... 70

When Love Hurts: Recognizing Dysfunctional Norms.. 73

PART III: REPAIR BEGINS WITHIN — THE INNER WORK... 77

Chapter 7: Awareness Is the First Repair Tool....... 78

Identifying Your Attachment Triggers................78

Rewriting Inner Scripts and Core Beliefs..........80

Creating Emotional Safety Within Yourself....... 83

Chapter 8: Emotional Rewiring Through Mindfulness and Somatic Tools.. 87

The Body's Memory of Attachment Trauma..... 87

Grounding, Breathing, and Reassociating Safety. 89

Integrating Cognitive and Somatic Awareness. 93

Chapter 9: Building Secure Internal Attachment.....96
    Reparenting the Inner Child..............................96
    Cultivating Self-Compassion and Emotional Containment..98
    Becoming the Secure Base You Never Had...101

PART IV: HEALING IN RELATIONSHIP CONTEXTS.....105
    Chapter 10: Communicating Needs Without Anxiety or Withdrawal...106
        How to Express Without Over-Explaining or Shutting Down..106
        Attachment-Informed Communication Techniques...109
        Repairing Misattunement Through Active Listening..112
    Chapter 11: Setting Boundaries Without Shame or Guilt...116
        Why Boundaries Are Essential for Safety and Respect..116
        Differentiating Avoidance from Healthy Limits 118
        Practicing Boundary-Setting With Love..........120
    Chapter 12: Rebuilding Intimacy and Trust...........124
        How to Tolerate Closeness Without Losing Yourself...124
        Slowly Earning and Granting Trust.................127
        The Role of Consistency and Emotional Availability..130

PART V: SUSTAINABLE GROWTH AND LASTING CONNECTIONS..133
    Chapter 13: Becoming Secure — Shifting from Pattern to Choice..134

    What Earned Secure Attachment Looks Like. 134

    Choosing Differently in Love and Conflict....... 136

    Identifying When You've Healed (And What's Next)... 139

Chapter 14: Navigating Attachment in Friendships and Families... 142

    Not Just Romantic: Attachment Shows Up Everywhere... 142

    Repairing with Parents, Siblings, and Adult Children... 144

    When to Engage, Disengage, or Forgive........ 147

Chapter 15: Future Relationships Built on Emotional Integrity... 150

    Red Flags vs. Growth Opportunities in New Relationships.. 150

    Maintaining Secure Attachment in Long-Term Love... 152

    Living Authentically and Loving From Wholeness 155

Preface

Why This Book Matters

It begins with a silence most people know far too well—the aching silence after an argument, the silent phone that doesn't ring, the partner who rolls away instead of reaching out. It's the quiet confusion of feeling too much or feeling nothing at all. The emptiness in relationships that should feel safe. The panic in moments that should feel close. The emotional shutdown that masquerades as calm control. This silence isn't just a lack of sound. It's the roar of unmet needs, buried fears, and a nervous system caught in the crossfire of love and survival.

This book was born from that silence.

For years, I watched individuals—bright, intelligent, well-meaning people—spiral through cycles of longing and withdrawal in their relationships. They clung when they wanted to let go. They ran when they wanted to stay. They blamed themselves for being "too much" or "not enough." They told themselves, *"If I just try harder, maybe they'll love me better"* or *"If I don't need anyone, no one can hurt me."* These are not uncommon thoughts. In fact, they are tragically familiar to anyone whose attachment style is shaped by anxious or avoidant tendencies. I knew these patterns intimately, both professionally and personally. And I knew how deeply they hurt.

When I began studying attachment theory in earnest, everything shifted. It was like someone had handed me the emotional blueprint I didn't know I'd lost. Suddenly, the behavior that once felt irrational made perfect sense. The need to check your partner's texts. The panic when they don't respond. The cold detachment when emotions surface. The walls that go up when someone gets too close. These weren't personality flaws or signs of emotional weakness. They were protective mechanisms—survival strategies crafted in childhood and carried like armor into adult relationships.

The more I worked with clients navigating these patterns, the more I saw how universal this struggle really was. People weren't failing at relationships because they were broken. They were stuck in attachment wounds that hadn't healed. And most had never been given the tools to understand, let alone repair, the ways they connected with others.

This book was written to change that.

It was written for the person who constantly feels "too much"—whose emotions rise like waves and crash without warning, who worries love will disappear the moment they turn their head. It's for the one who pulls away instead—who prides themselves on independence but secretly longs for someone to know them without needing to explain. It's for anyone whose relationships have felt like battlegrounds of closeness and distance, fear and desire, hope and heartbreak. And it's for those who want to change—not just to feel better temporarily, but to truly *heal*.

The Problem Is Not Who You Are—It's What You Learned to Do to Stay Safe
Attachment patterns are not life sentences. They are learned, not inherent. Which means they can also be unlearned, rewired, and transformed. But most people trying to "fix" their relationship problems don't realize that their issues don't start in the relationship itself—they begin in the nervous system. In the internal wiring that was shaped long before they chose their first partner. Until that wiring is understood and compassionately rewired, no amount of relationship advice will stick. Because the issue isn't just what you say—it's what your body believes about love, safety, and connection.

That's why traditional relationship advice often fails. You can read all the communication tips in the world. You can practice active listening, learn your love languages, and memorize conflict resolution strategies. But if your body still flinches at closeness—or panics at the hint of distance—those strategies will collapse under the weight of your attachment wounds. That's not your fault. It's not a character flaw. It's simply unaddressed attachment trauma playing out in real time.

What makes this book different is that it doesn't stop at the surface. It won't just teach you how to "communicate better" or "manage conflict." It will guide you deeper—into the roots of your emotional patterns, into the nervous system responses you didn't know you were having, into the childhood scripts you've been reenacting for decades. It will help you gently uncover what's driving your attachment style, not to judge yourself, but to reclaim power over your emotional life.

Because healing is not about fixing who you are—it's about returning to the secure self you were always meant to be.

A Journey of Recovery, Rewiring, and Connection
This book follows a clear arc: from understanding to awareness, from repair to transformation. It is divided into five parts, each one building on the last.

You will begin by understanding what attachment theory really is—not in vague psychological terms, but in emotionally lived reality. You'll learn how anxious and avoidant patterns develop, and why they continue to play out even in the face of logic or desire. You'll explore how these patterns show up in adult life—in conflict, intimacy, communication, and emotional regulation.

Then you'll move into the inner work. This is where transformation truly begins. You'll learn to recognize your emotional triggers, understand your nervous system's role in reactivity, and start to rewire the thought and behavior loops that keep you stuck. You'll discover the power of somatic tools—body-based practices that work directly with the limbic system, where attachment wounds are stored. You'll be guided to re-parent your inner child, develop self-compassion, and build internal emotional safety.

From there, the book will walk with you into the world of relationships. You'll learn how to express your needs without fear, set boundaries without guilt, and tolerate closeness without losing yourself. You'll discover how to build trust, repair ruptures, and choose relationships that support your growth. Whether you are in a relationship, healing from a breakup, or navigating the dating world, these tools will meet you where you are.

Finally, you'll learn how to sustain these changes. Because healing doesn't end with awareness—it deepens into embodiment. You'll explore what secure attachment looks like in action, how to maintain emotional balance, and how to recognize red flags before repeating old patterns. You'll be equipped to navigate not only romantic relationships, but friendships, family dynamics, and even your relationship with yourself, from a place of wholeness.

This Book Is for You—Even If You're Not Sure You're Ready
Maybe you're picking up this book at a low point—after yet another relationship ended in confusion or pain. Maybe you're in a relationship right now, but you feel like you're walking on eggshells, afraid to be fully seen. Or maybe you've distanced yourself from love altogether, deciding it's safer not to want what you've never been able to keep.

Wherever you are, this book meets you there. It doesn't ask you to have it all figured out. It only asks for your willingness to be honest, to be curious, and to believe—just a little—that change is possible.

You don't have to be perfect to heal. You don't have to be in a relationship to learn secure attachment. You don't need to "fix" your past before you can feel whole in the present. What you need is a roadmap, a compassionate guide, and tools that work—not just in theory, but in practice.

That's what this book offers.

A Word on Language and Compassion
Throughout this journey, you will not be pathologized or labeled. This is not a book that will call you broken, needy, or emotionally unavailable. Those labels do nothing but deepen shame. Instead, you will be met with compassionate understanding and informed, actionable steps. Attachment styles are *descriptions*, not *destinies*. They are a way to make sense of your experience—not a box to stay trapped in.

You will see stories, case studies, and real-life examples to help normalize your experience. You will be invited to reflect, not just read. You will be guided through exercises to rewire your patterns slowly, safely, and sustainably. And you will be supported in developing the skills you were never taught but deeply deserve—emotional safety, effective communication, healthy boundaries, and secure connection.

This is not self-help fluff. It's nervous-system-informed, psychologically sound, heart-centered work.

What You'll Walk Away With

By the end of this book, you will have:

- A clear understanding of your attachment style and how it developed
- Insight into how your style impacts your thoughts, emotions, and relationships
- Tools to regulate your emotions and calm your nervous system
- Scripts and strategies to communicate needs without shame or fear
- Techniques for boundary-setting that respect both yourself and others
- A framework for identifying healthy, secure relationships
- Guidance for building lasting emotional intimacy—without losing yourself
- Hope. Not just abstract hope, but *grounded, practical, daily* hope

Healing anxious and avoidant attachment is not about becoming someone else. It's about coming home to who you truly are—someone worthy of love, capable of giving and receiving it, and resilient enough to grow through every challenge.

If you've ever wondered, *"Will I ever feel truly safe in love?"*

If you've ever feared that you are "too much" or "not enough"…

If you've ever longed for a relationship where you don't have to earn your worth…

This book is your answer.

You are not broken.
You are not unlovable.
You are not doomed to repeat the past.

You are healing.
You are rewiring.
You are returning to a secure connection—one page, one choice, one breath at a time.

Welcome to your new path.
Let's begin.

Introduction: A New Path to Emotional Security

Emotional security. The phrase itself might sound foreign if you've never truly felt it. For many, it doesn't bring to mind the warmth of steady love, the calm of knowing you're safe, or the relief of being understood without defense. Instead, it stirs confusion—*What does that even feel like? Is it even real?* For those with anxious or avoidant attachment patterns, emotional security may have always felt just out of reach. And yet, it is the very foundation upon which stable, loving relationships are built.

This book is a roadmap back to that foundation. But before you can rebuild anything, you have to understand what made it crack in the first place.

The Problem with Traditional Relationship Advice

Walk into any bookstore or scroll through relationship advice online, and you'll find an endless stream of guidance: "Just communicate your needs," "Learn your partner's love language," "Stop being so clingy," "Let them miss you," "Don't take it personally," "Stay mysterious." Much of it comes from well-meaning sources. Some of it even sounds helpful at first glance. But for someone struggling with insecure attachment, these tips don't just fall flat—they often make things worse.

Why? Because they address the *behavior*, not the *cause*. They assume that everyone begins a relationship on even emotional ground, that love is only about skills and choices. But insecure attachment runs deeper than that. It isn't about strategy—it's about survival. It's not that you *won't* relax, trust, or communicate clearly. It's that your *body won't let you*. Your nervous system has learned that closeness equals threat, or that distance equals abandonment, and it acts accordingly—often without your permission.

So when traditional advice tells you to "just trust" or "be less needy," it ignores the reality of your nervous system's programming. It skips over the years—often decades—of unmet needs, inconsistent caregivers, emotional neglect, or trauma that shaped how you love and fear love. That's not something you override with logic or positive thinking. It's something that needs to be gently rewired, from the inside out.

Here's what most advice doesn't tell you: You're not broken. You're not failing at relationships because you lack discipline or insight. You're doing what your emotional system was wired to do—protect you from pain, abandonment, or engulfment. The problem is that what once protected you may now be keeping you from the connection you long for.

This book isn't just a new collection of strategies. It's a new paradigm—one that honors your past without letting it define your future.

What Emotional Security *Actually* Feels Like

Emotional security is not about perfection. It doesn't mean you'll never argue, never feel scared, never get triggered. It means that even in the midst of conflict or fear, you don't lose your sense of self. It means you can express your needs without believing you'll be rejected for having them. It means you can let someone in without needing to know how the story ends. It means that love no longer feels like walking a tightrope between closeness and collapse.

For the anxiously attached, emotional security feels like this:

You no longer chase reassurance because you already believe in your worth.

You don't beg for scraps of affection or silence your voice just to stay close.

You know how to calm the panic that once made you cling, overthink, or self-abandon.

For the avoidantly attached, emotional security feels like this:

You no longer see intimacy as a threat to your freedom.

You don't pull away the moment someone gets too close or demands emotional presence.

You learn that interdependence is not weakness—it's strength.

For both, it's about finally coming home to yourself. It's about being able to stay present, even when love feels unfamiliar. It's about trusting that you can handle connection, not because it will always be easy, but because you've built the capacity to stay emotionally safe, even in discomfort.

You might be wondering: *Is that even possible for me?* Yes. Not only is it possible—it's within reach. But it doesn't come through tricks or fast fixes. It comes through deep, inner repair.

The Promise of the Work Ahead

If you've made it this far, you're already doing something most people never do: you're looking inward instead of outward. That alone is the beginning of transformation.

This book will not promise you a perfect relationship. But it *will* promise this: if you commit to this work, you will stop abandoning yourself. You will stop outsourcing your worth. You will stop letting fear masquerade as self-protection. And you will start to build a new emotional foundation—one based not on survival, but on safety, choice, and connection.

Over the course of this book, you'll gain:

- **Clarity**: about your patterns, your past, and how they've shaped your present
- **Awareness**: of the specific emotional and physiological triggers that send you into attachment spirals
- **Tools**: for calming your nervous system, expressing your needs, and forming secure bonds

- **Empowerment**: to stop repeating old cycles and start choosing relationships that nourish rather than deplete you

You'll explore the anatomy of attachment theory, but more importantly, you'll see how it plays out in your day-to-day life—how it affects how you text, how you argue, how you cope, and how you connect.

You'll be asked to confront some uncomfortable truths: that love isn't supposed to feel like anxiety. That walls aren't protection, they're isolation. That neediness isn't weakness, and that detachment isn't strength. These truths might hurt at first, but only because they shine light on places you've kept hidden for so long.

But you'll also be given powerful new truths to hold:
That you can feel deeply *and* stay grounded.
That you can ask for what you need without fear of being too much.
That you can let someone in without losing yourself.
That you can unlearn what hurt you and relearn what heals.

This is not a quick fix book. This is a companion for long-term healing. That means there will be moments where the work feels hard. You might want to put the book down. You might think, *"Maybe I'm just not cut out for this."* But that's not your truth. That's your attachment wound speaking. And part of the healing is learning to recognize that voice and gently tell it: *"I hear you. But I'm choosing something different now."*

You are not alone in this process. The pages ahead are designed to walk with you, not push you. You'll find stories from others who've lived through similar struggles. You'll find exercises that help your body integrate what your mind is learning. You'll be asked to reflect, but you'll also be equipped to act. To make small, powerful shifts. To move from fear to understanding, from reaction to intention, from protection to presence.

And no matter how you begin, you will end in a place of greater strength, stability, and security than you thought possible.

A Different Kind of Love Story
This isn't just a book about relationships. It's a book about *you*. About your emotional blueprint. Your nervous system. Your unmet needs. Your defense mechanisms. Your capacity to love and be loved.

But more than that, it's a book about reclaiming something sacred: your right to feel safe in love.

So many of us are taught that love is supposed to hurt, or that it's normal to feel constantly anxious, distant, or exhausted in our connections. We normalize suffering in the name of romance. We confuse intensity with intimacy. We think being wanted means being worthy.

But love, at its core, is supposed to feel safe. That doesn't mean it's always easy. It means that even in difficulty, there's a shared sense of commitment, respect, and emotional presence.

Secure attachment is the soil from which that kind of love grows.

And your healing is the seed.

Let this book be the start of a different kind of love story—not one where you're saved by another person, but one where you learn to meet yourself fully, love yourself deeply, and choose partners who honor that love.

Let this be the moment you stop performing for love. Stop shrinking. Stop chasing. Stop shutting down. Start feeling. Start staying. Start connecting.

You don't have to repeat the past. You don't have to wait for someone else to "complete" you. You are whole, worthy, and enough—right now. The only thing left is to remember that, and to live from it.

This is your new path.
 Let's walk it together.

PART I: UNDERSTANDING ATTACHMENT — THE ROOT OF RELATIONSHIP STRUGGLES

Chapter 1: What Is Attachment Theory, Really?

The Science Behind Early Bonds

Human beings are not born into the world as emotionally self-sufficient entities. From the very beginning, we are wired to seek closeness, comfort, and protection. A newborn does not survive without connection; in fact, even beyond physical nourishment, infants require emotional and neurological attunement to thrive. This biological imperative forms the bedrock of what is known as **attachment theory**—the idea that our earliest interactions with caregivers shape not only how we connect to others but also how we regulate emotions, handle stress, and develop a sense of self.

Attachment theory was originally developed by British psychologist **John Bowlby**, who believed that a child's bond with their primary caregiver serves as the internal model for future relationships. Bowlby argued that this attachment system is instinctive, driven by evolution to keep the infant close to their caregiver for survival. However, beyond physical safety, this bond also provides *emotional safety*. When that emotional bond is secure—when the caregiver is consistently responsive and attuned—the child learns that the world is a safe place, that others can be trusted, and that they are worthy of love.

Later, psychologist **Mary Ainsworth** expanded on Bowlby's work through a series of observational studies known as the **Strange Situation** experiments. Her research revealed that the way a child reacts to separation and reunion with their caregiver offers insight into their underlying attachment pattern. These patterns, she found, were not random but deeply predictive of how individuals would later approach relationships, intimacy, independence, and vulnerability.

What makes attachment theory so powerful is that it bridges developmental psychology, neuroscience, and interpersonal relationships. It explains why we behave the way we do in moments of closeness or conflict. Why some people seek reassurance while others pull away. Why vulnerability feels safe for some and threatening for others. And most importantly, it reveals that these tendencies are not flaws—they are adaptations.

From a neurobiological perspective, attachment experiences get encoded in the brain's limbic system—the emotional brain—particularly during the formative early years. The caregiver's responsiveness, or lack thereof, shapes the development of the child's **amygdala** (which governs fear), **hippocampus** (which regulates memory and emotional context), and **prefrontal cortex** (responsible for emotional regulation and decision-making). If a child consistently experiences comfort, regulation, and warmth in moments of distress, the neural pathways formed around connection and safety become stable. If they experience neglect, inconsistency, or intrusion, the emotional brain wires itself around survival, not trust.

This early wiring becomes the *blueprint* for future relational behavior. It forms what Bowlby called the **internal working model**—an unconscious template for understanding the self (*Am I lovable?*), others (*Can I rely on others?*), and the world (*Is it safe to be open?*). This internal model operates beneath the level of conscious awareness, influencing every relationship dynamic in adulthood, from how we interpret our partner's tone of voice to how we react when someone pulls away emotionally.

Crucially, this internal model is *not* fixed. Although shaped in early childhood, it remains *plastic*—capable of change through conscious reflection, corrective emotional experiences, therapy, and intentional relational work. That is where the promise of healing comes in. But before we explore how to repair attachment wounds, we must first understand the styles in which these wounds typically manifest.

The Four Major Attachment Styles Explained
Most people enter adulthood with a predominant attachment style that shapes how they give and receive love. While human behavior is complex and often fluid, attachment styles offer a useful framework for understanding recurring emotional patterns. These styles are not moral judgments or rigid labels—they are adaptive strategies developed in response to early caregiving environments.

There are **four primary attachment styles**: *secure, anxious (also known as preoccupied), avoidant (also* *known as dismissive)*, and *disorganized (also known as fearful-avoidant)*. Each reflects a different relational blueprint—how we manage closeness, interpret others' intentions, and regulate our emotional needs.

1. Secure Attachment
A secure attachment style is the result of consistent, responsive caregiving. These individuals were emotionally attuned to as children. They learned that their needs would be met, their emotions were valid, and connection was safe.

In adult relationships, securely attached individuals are typically:

- Comfortable with emotional intimacy
- Able to express their needs directly
- Trusting without being overly dependent
- Able to balance autonomy and closeness

Securely attached individuals are not without conflict, but they approach it with openness rather than fear. They assume goodwill in others, recover quickly from relational stress, and seek resolution rather than withdrawal or escalation.

2. Anxious Attachment (Preoccupied Style)
Anxious attachment develops in children whose caregivers were inconsistent—sometimes loving, sometimes emotionally unavailable. These children learned that attention must be earned or maintained through vigilance, emotional intensity, or hyper-attunement to others' moods.

As adults, people with an anxious attachment style often:

- Crave closeness but fear abandonment
- Overanalyze partners' behavior for signs of rejection
- Require frequent reassurance
- Feel unworthy of love and prone to self-blame

Anxiously attached individuals often feel that they care more than their partner, which triggers insecurity and protest behaviors such as clinging, guilt-tripping, or emotional outbursts. Their relationships can feel intense but unstable, driven by the fear of being left or not being enough.

3. Avoidant Attachment (Dismissive Style)
Avoidant attachment stems from early environments where emotional needs were dismissed, punished, or ignored. These children learned that vulnerability led to rejection or shame, so they internalized a message: *don't need, don't feel, don't depend*.

In adulthood, avoidantly attached individuals often:

- Value independence over closeness
- Have difficulty expressing emotions
- Minimize the importance of relationships
- Detach or shut down during emotional conflict

They may appear self-sufficient or emotionally strong, but beneath the surface lies a deep discomfort with intimacy. They fear engulfment, so they manage relationships by staying emotionally distant. This can confuse or frustrate partners who seek connection.

4. Disorganized Attachment (Fearful-Avoidant Style)
Disorganized attachment typically develops in children who experienced trauma, neglect, or chaotic caregiving. Their caregivers were sources of both comfort and fear. This creates a paradox in which the child seeks closeness but simultaneously feels unsafe in connection.

In adulthood, individuals with disorganized attachment may:

- Swing between clinginess and emotional withdrawal
- Experience high anxiety and high avoidance
- Struggle with self-worth, trust, and emotional regulation
- Engage in push-pull dynamics or self-sabotage

This style reflects profound relational confusion: *I want love, but love hurts*. Healing for disorganized attachment requires both trauma-informed care and gradual emotional re-integration.

It's important to note that attachment styles are **not diagnoses**. They are descriptions of how people respond to emotional stimuli in relationships. Many people exhibit traits from more than one style, or shift styles depending on the context or partner. The goal is not to rigidly identify yourself as "anxious" or "avoidant" forever—it's to understand your tendencies so you can begin the work of healing.

And that healing starts with a fundamental shift in how we understand ourselves and others.

Why Understanding This Changes Everything

When someone first learns about attachment theory, it often lands with a sense of profound clarity: *Oh, so that's why I always do that.* It reframes what felt like irrational behavior into understandable, predictable responses rooted in survival. That understanding alone can be transformational. Because once you understand your attachment style, you no longer have to live at the mercy of it.

Here's why this insight is so powerful: it shifts the focus from *what's wrong with me?* to *what happened to me—and what did I learn from it?* This distinction is everything.

If you believe your relationship struggles stem from being "too emotional" or "cold-hearted," you're likely to fall into shame, self-judgment, and hopelessness. But if you realize that your behaviors were once intelligent strategies to manage inconsistent caregiving or emotional neglect, you can start to hold yourself with compassion. You can see that your fears of abandonment or intimacy aren't signs of brokenness. They are signs of *adaptation*. And anything that was learned—can be unlearned.

Moreover, attachment theory empowers you to stop trying to "fix" the other person and start focusing on your own internal healing. Instead of asking, *How do I make them stay?* or *How do I make them open up?* you begin asking, *How do I create emotional safety within myself, so I no longer need to chase or run from connection?*

This internal shift also changes how you interpret relational dynamics. For example:

- When an anxious person sees delayed replies as rejection, they can now pause and ask, *Is this my wound speaking, or is something actually wrong?*
- When an avoidant partner feels smothered by emotional closeness, they can explore where that discomfort began, instead of withdrawing without explanation.
- When two insecurely attached people trigger each other's wounds, they can begin to recognize the cycle rather than blame each other.

Understanding attachment styles also fosters **empathy**. When you know your partner's attachment style, you can begin to see their behavior not as a personal attack but as a protective adaptation. The anxious partner's "neediness" becomes a call for reassurance, not manipulation. The avoidant's "coldness" becomes an attempt to self-regulate, not rejection. The disorganized partner's chaos becomes a survival response, not cruelty.

This understanding doesn't excuse harmful behavior—but it helps you respond with curiosity instead of condemnation. And that opens the door for real repair.

Finally, understanding attachment changes how you love yourself. Most of us inherited our relational patterns without choice. But healing gives us back the agency to choose again. To relate from a place of wholeness, not wounds. To create love that doesn't demand performance or perfection, but invites presence and honesty.

Attachment theory is not just about relationships. It's about **freedom**. Freedom from unconscious cycles. Freedom from fear. Freedom to connect, to be vulnerable, to stay present, and to love well.

And that freedom begins now.

Chapter 2: Anxious Attachment — The Fear of Abandonment

Origins in Childhood Dynamics

To understand anxious attachment in adulthood, we must return to the earliest years of life—the crucible in which the attachment system is formed. For those with an anxious attachment style, early relationships were marked by emotional inconsistency. Caregivers were sometimes loving and attentive, and other times distracted, distant, critical, or emotionally unavailable. This unpredictability taught the child a dangerous lesson: *Love is not a given. It must be earned. And it can disappear at any moment.*

An infant is not capable of interpreting their caregiver's inconsistency. A distracted or emotionally overwhelmed parent may not realize the impact of missed emotional attunement, but for the developing child, these lapses become deeply encoded. The child doesn't yet have language or logic, only a felt sense of *something is missing*. In a secure environment, the child experiences consistent soothing during moments of distress—when they cry, someone comes; when they are hurt, someone comforts. This consistency builds a secure base from which the child learns to explore the world, confident in the knowledge that their caregiver is a safe and reliable source of comfort.

For a child developing anxious attachment, this base is shaky. Sometimes the caregiver responds with warmth. Other times, they may ignore, shame, or become agitated by the child's emotional expression. Inconsistent affection creates confusion: *Will I be held or rejected? Will my sadness be comforted or punished?* The child becomes hypervigilant, scanning constantly for cues of attention or abandonment. This is not a conscious choice—it is a survival mechanism. If love and safety are intermittent, the child learns to amplify their emotional expression in order to secure the caregiver's focus.

This pattern hardens over time. As the child matures, they may become clingy, emotionally intense, or overly accommodating. Their sense of self becomes entangled with the emotional availability of the caregiver. When love is present, they feel valuable. When it is withdrawn, they feel unworthy. They begin to form an internal working model that says: *I am only lovable when I perform. I must monitor and manage others' emotions to feel safe. If someone pulls away, it's because I've done something wrong.*

These early beliefs, though formed in childhood, are rarely updated. The child grows into an adult who still operates from the same emotional logic. The people around them may change, but the blueprint remains: *love is fragile, and I must work to keep it from disappearing.*

Not all anxious attachment styles emerge from overt trauma or abuse. Often, these dynamics arise in households that seem functional on the surface. A parent who is physically present but emotionally preoccupied—perhaps due to their own unhealed wounds, stress, depression, or cultural norms around emotional expression—can unintentionally foster anxious attachment. What matters most is not how much love a parent *feels*, but how consistently that love is *felt* by the child.

In these environments, the child's nervous system becomes sensitized to relational threat. They may grow up appearing socially capable and outwardly confident, but internally, they carry an ongoing fear: *People I love might leave me. I am too much. I need others to feel okay.*

This early fear—of abandonment, rejection, or emotional invisibility—becomes the core wound that shapes adult anxious attachment. And it doesn't disappear just because someone grows up. Instead, it finds new ways to express itself in intimate relationships, often causing distress, confusion, and a hunger for reassurance that never seems fully satisfied.

Common Behaviors in Adult Relationships
In adulthood, the anxious attachment style surfaces in emotionally charged patterns that center around one core belief: *My connection with others is always at risk, and it's my job to protect it.* This underlying fear creates behaviors that, while understandable and even logical to the person exhibiting them, often appear overwhelming, confusing, or frustrating to partners.

Anxiously attached individuals are often highly attuned to emotional shifts. They notice the slight change in a partner's tone, the delayed text response, the subtle withdrawal after an argument. To someone with a secure attachment style, these cues might be dismissed or explained away. But to the anxiously attached person, these shifts are red flags—signs that love is slipping away. And because the internal belief is *I must act to preserve connection*, they respond in ways that attempt to pull the partner closer.

These behaviors may include:

- **Frequent seeking of reassurance**: Anxious individuals often need to hear, sometimes daily, that they are loved, wanted, and safe in the relationship. This is not manipulation—it is emotional survival. Without reassurance, the internal panic grows. They may ask questions like, "Do you still love me?" or "Are you mad at me?" not because they doubt the partner's past affection, but because their sense of emotional security resets to zero at every perceived disconnection.
- **Overanalysis and rumination**: Small relational cues become magnified. A one-word reply can spiral into hours of inner dialogue. "What did I say wrong?" "Why didn't they use a heart emoji this time?" This obsessive thinking is an attempt to gain control over what feels like an emotionally unsafe environment.

- **Over-functioning**: Many anxiously attached people believe that if they give more, please more, or do more, their partner won't leave. They may overextend themselves emotionally, suppress their own needs, or constantly try to manage the partner's feelings. While this may temporarily maintain connection, it leads to exhaustion, resentment, and the erosion of self.
- **Fear of being alone**: Anxious individuals may struggle with breakups, even in unhealthy relationships, because disconnection feels like annihilation. They may stay in situations that harm them, not because they lack awareness, but because the fear of abandonment overrides the pain of mistreatment.
- **Emotional reactivity**: When a perceived threat to connection arises, the anxiously attached person may become emotionally escalated—crying, protesting, or becoming angry. These reactions are not meant to hurt the partner; they are driven by a sense of urgent distress: *I need to know I'm not being abandoned right now.*

These behaviors are often misunderstood. Partners may label them as "needy," "dramatic," or "clingy." But beneath them lies a fragile emotional nervous system, shaped by years of uncertainty and unmet needs. The anxious partner is not trying to control—they are trying to soothe a deep, unrelenting fear.

Ironically, the very behaviors meant to preserve connection can sometimes push others away. This is especially true in relationships where one partner is avoidantly attached. The anxious person's intensity triggers the avoidant's fear of engulfment, causing them to withdraw, which only heightens the anxious person's panic. This creates the classic "pursuer-distancer" dynamic—a painful cycle in which both individuals are trying to protect themselves, but inadvertently reinforce each other's fears.

Yet, when these patterns are brought into awareness, they can be interrupted and healed. The first step is understanding the emotional feedback loops that keep the anxious attachment system activated.

Emotional Triggers and Reinforcement Loops
The anxious attachment style is kept alive not just by past experiences but by the ongoing **emotional reinforcement loops** it creates in the present. These loops are like relational scripts—trigger, response, panic, attempt to soothe, momentary relief, and reset. They operate beneath conscious awareness, shaping how the individual reacts to intimacy, distance, and emotional ambiguity.

Understanding these loops is critical for breaking the cycle of anxiety-driven behavior.

Let's begin with **triggers**. A trigger is not just a big fight or a breakup. For someone with anxious attachment, it can be as subtle as:

- A partner being quieter than usual
- Not receiving a reply to a message within a "normal" time
- A change in facial expression or tone
- A canceled plan
- A perceived shift in attention or affection

These triggers activate the internal alarm system: *Something's wrong. I'm being pushed away. I might be abandoned.* The brain, trained by years of early emotional instability, interprets these signals as threats, even if no actual rejection is occurring.

This perception leads to **emotional responses** such as panic, overthinking, or a flood of fear. The body enters a fight-or-flight state—heart rate increases, breath shortens, muscles tense. The mind races to interpret the situation and protect itself. This is where anxious individuals often engage in **protest behaviors**—calling repeatedly, sending multiple messages, picking a fight, becoming excessively apologetic, or making exaggerated gestures to win back the partner's attention.

When the partner eventually responds—through reassurance, reconnection, or even conflict resolution—the anxious individual feels momentarily soothed. The nervous system calms down. The fear recedes. But instead of dismantling the loop, this pattern actually **reinforces** it. The brain learns: *When I panic and protest, connection is restored.* And so, the next time there's a perceived threat, the same response is activated.

These cycles are exhausting—for both the anxious individual and their partner. But they are not chosen consciously. They are learned responses to emotional unpredictability. The anxious brain is not trying to create drama—it is trying to survive what feels like emotional life or death.

The challenge is that these loops can become *self-fulfilling*. Constant checking and emotional protests may strain the relationship, causing the partner to withdraw, which confirms the anxious person's fear: *I knew they were pulling away.* This deepens the belief that love is unstable, that they are "too much," and that connection must always be fought for.

To break these loops, awareness is key. The anxious individual must begin to distinguish between real threats and perceived ones. They must learn to **self-soothe**, to regulate their nervous system before seeking reassurance, and to develop internal safety that doesn't depend entirely on another person's behavior. This doesn't mean ignoring needs—it means grounding in the present before responding from past wounds.

The healing journey involves gently interrupting the cycle at multiple points:

- Noticing the trigger and naming it
- Pausing before reacting

- Breathing into the discomfort rather than immediately reaching outward
- Choosing new ways to respond—asking for reassurance calmly, validating your own feelings, staying anchored in the present moment

Over time, with practice, support, and sometimes professional guidance, the anxious attachment system can be **rewired**. The goal is not to become emotionally numb or hyper-independent, but to move toward a secure attachment style—where needs are expressed with confidence, where closeness feels safe, and where connection no longer has to be earned through anxiety.

The fear of abandonment does not have to define your relationships forever. It is not your identity. It is a wound. And wounds can heal.

The next chapter explores the opposite side of the attachment spectrum—**Avoidant Attachment**, where emotional distance, not closeness, becomes the survival strategy. Understanding both sides of the attachment divide is essential for building bridges to secure, lasting connections.

Chapter 3: Avoidant Attachment — The Fear of Intimacy

Disconnection as a Coping Mechanism

For those with avoidant attachment, intimacy often feels less like a comfort and more like a threat. While the anxious person fears abandonment, the avoidant person fears enmeshment. They carry an internal belief that closeness will lead to a loss of control, autonomy, or even identity. These individuals learned, often very early in life, that emotional independence was not only preferred—it was necessary.

In childhood, the avoidant pattern usually develops in environments where emotional needs were not met consistently or where vulnerability was discouraged, dismissed, or punished. The child quickly learns that expressing distress does not bring comfort. Crying may be met with irritation. Anger may result in withdrawal. Sadness may be minimized or ignored. In such an environment, the child's nervous system adapts—not by seeking more connection, but by suppressing the need for it altogether.

This suppression is not a sign of resilience. It is a trauma response. The child disconnects from their emotional world to preserve the attachment to a caregiver who cannot or will not meet their emotional needs. Rather than risk rejection, the child chooses detachment. It is safer to not need, not feel, not want—because then there is no risk of disappointment.

This disconnection becomes habitual. The child grows into an adult who believes that relying on others is a liability. They may pride themselves on being "low maintenance" or "independent," but beneath the surface lies a deep mistrust of emotional closeness. Intimacy becomes synonymous with vulnerability, and vulnerability feels dangerous.

Avoidantly attached individuals often don't remember their childhoods as emotionally neglectful. In fact, many describe their upbringing as "fine," "normal," or "good." The pain wasn't always visible or dramatic. Sometimes, it was the subtle, chronic absence of warmth—a parent who provided structure and discipline but not attunement or tenderness. Other times, it was a culture or household where stoicism and emotional restraint were seen as strengths, and expression of feelings was considered weak or indulgent.

The result is a child who grows into an adult with a restricted emotional vocabulary and a heightened sensitivity to emotional demands. They may find emotional closeness suffocating, not because they don't want love, but because they were never given the tools to engage with it safely.

In relationships, this disconnection becomes the dominant coping mechanism. When faced with conflict, neediness, or emotional intensity, the avoidantly attached person withdraws. They retreat into themselves. They shut down rather than reach out. And while this withdrawal may appear cold or dismissive to their partners, it is actually a form of self-preservation. The avoidant person is trying to manage overwhelming feelings by creating space—because space is what once kept them safe.

Avoidant individuals are not without feelings. They simply learned to disassociate from them early. They do not lack the capacity for love—they lack trust in the process of emotional intimacy. Their distance is not cruelty—it is fear.

Understanding this origin is crucial. Because without compassion for the avoidant's coping mechanism, it is easy to judge, criticize, or abandon them in their emotional detachment. But with understanding, the door opens to healing—to helping the avoidant person reconnect with their emotional self and with others in a way that feels safe, gradual, and authentic.

Emotional Suppression and Self-Sufficiency
If anxious attachment creates emotional intensity and protest, avoidant attachment does the opposite—it creates emotional suppression and pseudo-self-sufficiency. These individuals often present as calm, composed, and in control. They are rarely overwhelmed by emotion—because they rarely allow themselves to feel it.

Avoidant individuals may describe themselves as "rational," "independent," or "logical." They are often uncomfortable with displays of vulnerability—either in themselves or others. Crying, deep emotional conversations, or expressions of need may trigger discomfort, defensiveness, or withdrawal. In many cases, they may not even register their own emotional states until they are physically exhausted, overwhelmed, or distant beyond repair.

This suppression is deeply neurological. Studies show that individuals with avoidant attachment have reduced activity in brain areas associated with emotional awareness. They are less attuned to bodily signals (interoception) and often struggle to identify what they are feeling. Ask an avoidantly attached person how they feel, and they might pause—not because they are hiding something, but because the question itself doesn't register as meaningful.

This emotional disconnect often translates into **self-sufficiency**—a belief that *I can and should handle everything on my own*. Relying on others feels risky. Depending on a partner feels unsafe. The avoidant individual may go to great lengths to avoid situations that make them feel vulnerable—whether it's asking for help, admitting they're hurt, or allowing someone to see their inner world.

In relationships, this creates specific patterns:

- **Keeping emotional distance**: They may keep conversations surface-level or intellectual to avoid emotional depth.

- **Minimizing problems**: When issues arise, they may downplay them, dismiss concerns, or avoid discussion altogether.
- **Withdrawing under stress**: Conflict or emotional intensity often leads to physical or emotional withdrawal.
- **Delayed processing**: They may need extended time to process feelings, often retreating to solitude without explaining why.

To their partners, this behavior can feel like rejection or emotional abandonment. But to the avoidant individual, it is often the only way they know how to stay regulated. Intimacy triggers internal alarms: *If I let you in, I'll lose control. If I depend on you, I'll be hurt.* So they maintain distance, not out of malice, but from learned protection.

Ironically, many avoidant individuals long for connection. They desire love, partnership, and intimacy—but their nervous system equates closeness with danger. This creates an internal contradiction: *I want to be close, but closeness overwhelms me. I want to be seen, but I fear judgment. I want support, but I don't know how to receive it.*

This internal struggle is rarely voiced. Instead, avoidant individuals may seek relationships with emotionally expressive partners (often those with anxious attachment), unconsciously hoping the other person will carry the emotional load. At first, this works. The anxious partner gives, initiates, and pursues. The avoidant partner receives, withdraws, and maintains autonomy. But over time, both feel unmet. The anxious person feels abandoned. The avoidant person feels pressured.

Breaking this cycle requires helping the avoidant individual build emotional literacy, develop tolerance for vulnerability, and gently challenge the belief that intimacy equals engulfment. It involves learning to feel—without being overwhelmed. To stay present—even when it's uncomfortable. And to reframe self-sufficiency not as a wall, but as a strength that can now be balanced with mutual support.

The journey is not about forcing openness. It's about creating emotional safety—so that openness becomes possible.

How Avoidance Shapes Romantic and Social Bonds

The avoidant attachment style doesn't exist in isolation. It plays out in real-time across romantic, platonic, and even professional relationships—shaping how these individuals form bonds, maintain boundaries, and navigate emotional closeness.

In romantic relationships, avoidant individuals often:

- Prefer low-maintenance partners or emotionally self-contained people
- Avoid "drama" or deep emotional processing

- Have difficulty expressing love or appreciation in verbal or emotional ways
- Need significant time alone to recharge
- Feel smothered by constant communication or emotional demands
- Exit relationships abruptly when things become "too serious"

They may appear to "fall out of love" quickly or detach easily. But often, this is not a lack of love—it's an overwhelmed nervous system shutting down. Love that asks them to feel deeply, express needs, or share vulnerability activates the early fear: *This is too much. I'm losing myself. I need to escape.* And so they retreat, not always because the relationship is wrong, but because their emotional wiring cannot yet tolerate the closeness.

In friendships, avoidantly attached individuals may be seen as reliable but emotionally unavailable. They are often loyal, helpful, and stable, but hesitant to share personal struggles. They may listen but not disclose. They prefer activity-based interactions over emotional sharing. This makes them valued friends in some circles, but difficult to reach on a deeper level.

In family relationships, avoidance may take the form of distance, emotional neutrality, or conflict avoidance. Conversations stay on safe topics. Emotional pain is kept private. Family obligations may be fulfilled dutifully, but without warmth or intimacy.

Even in professional environments, avoidant patterns can emerge. These individuals often excel in solo work, leadership, or structured roles. They are independent, focused, and effective. But they may avoid conflict, struggle with feedback, or resist collaborative environments where emotional dynamics are present.

Despite this widespread impact, avoidantly attached individuals often don't recognize their own patterns. Because they are not "overreacting" or visibly distressed, their coping mechanisms are often praised. They are seen as composed, rational, or strong. But beneath the surface, many feel isolated, unseen, or emotionally unfulfilled. Their lives may be organized—but emotionally disconnected.

Healing avoidant attachment involves more than learning how to talk about feelings. It requires building emotional tolerance slowly, honoring the nervous system's limits, and expanding the window of intimacy in safe, incremental ways. It involves redefining closeness—not as a threat, but as a source of nourishment.

For avoidant individuals, the goal is not to become emotionally enmeshed or dependent. The goal is integration: to stay emotionally present, even when it's uncomfortable. To express affection without fear of engulfment. To allow others in—not because you need them to complete you, but because connection, when secure, can be a safe and enriching part of life.

Avoidant attachment is not a flaw—it's an adaptation. But it no longer has to be your only strategy. You can build new ways of relating—ways that honor your independence *and* welcome intimacy. This book will guide you in doing just that.

PART II: THE COST OF INSECURE ATTACHMENT IN ADULT LIFE

Chapter 4: The Push-Pull Dance in Relationships

Why Anxious and Avoidant Partners Often Attract
The dance between anxious and avoidant partners is one of the most common and confusing dynamics in adult relationships. On the surface, these two attachment styles seem like opposites—one seeks closeness while the other avoids it. But beneath the contrast lies a magnetic pull, a paradoxical attraction that often brings them together and, just as often, pulls them painfully apart.

The anxious partner, deeply attuned to shifts in emotional availability, is drawn to the avoidant partner's independence, calm demeanor, and seeming emotional self-sufficiency. In the early stages of a relationship, the avoidant person may appear grounded and even romantic in their measured way, providing the anxious partner with an illusion of safety and stability. For someone accustomed to emotional chaos, the avoidant's reserve can feel like a relief.

The avoidant partner, on the other hand, often finds the anxious partner's warmth, openness, and emotional expressiveness compelling—at least initially. They may admire the anxious person's passion and devotion, especially when they themselves struggle to access emotional depth. The attention and intensity can feel flattering, even comforting. The anxious partner seems willing to carry the emotional load—at least for a while.

This mutual fascination, however, is built on unmet needs that remain unspoken. The anxious partner yearns for deep emotional connection and constant reassurance. The avoidant partner values space, autonomy, and emotional distance. While each partner is drawn to the qualities the other appears to offer, both are also terrified by what the other represents.

For the anxious partner, the avoidant's tendency to detach activates their deepest fears: *I am not enough. I am being abandoned.* For the avoidant, the anxious partner's need for closeness triggers an equally deep fear: *I'm being consumed. I'm losing myself.*

The result is a painful cycle. The anxious person pursues connection, asking for more time, more affection, more emotional presence. The avoidant partner, feeling pressured and overwhelmed, pulls away. The anxious person, sensing withdrawal, protests louder, increasing the pressure. The avoidant withdraws further, and the anxious partner panics. What began as attraction turns into reactivity, leaving both individuals feeling misunderstood and emotionally unsafe.

This dance isn't just frustrating—it's reenacting emotional blueprints learned in childhood. The anxious person, used to inconsistency and unpredictability, tries to prevent abandonment by becoming hyper-vigilant and emotionally accommodating. The avoidant person, used to emotional self-reliance, copes with intimacy by suppressing needs and distancing from emotion. Each partner unknowingly validates the other's core fear.

And yet, they often stay. Why?

Because both are, in different ways, seeking healing. The anxious partner wants to be chosen and made to feel secure. The avoidant partner wants to be loved without being swallowed. On a subconscious level, each is hoping the other will finally give them what their childhood did not—a stable, safe, emotionally attuned relationship.

Unfortunately, unless both partners become conscious of these dynamics and begin the work of self-regulation and repair, the cycle continues. What began as chemistry turns into chronic misattunement.

But the cycle is not inevitable. It can be interrupted—if both partners are willing to see what's really happening beneath the surface, and if each takes responsibility for their own healing.

Co-dependency, Distancing, and Misattunement
The push-pull cycle is often driven by the interplay of co-dependency, distancing behaviors, and emotional misattunement. To fully understand this dynamic, we must look more closely at how each partner contributes to the pattern—not in blame, but in compassionate awareness.

Co-dependency and the Anxious Partner
Co-dependency is a term that has been widely misunderstood. It doesn't mean simply caring too much—it refers to an emotional reliance on another person's validation and presence to feel stable or whole. In the context of anxious attachment, co-dependency often manifests as:

- Monitoring the partner's mood or behavior to determine one's emotional state
- Suppressing personal needs to avoid conflict or abandonment
- Feeling responsible for maintaining the emotional temperature of the relationship
- Requiring excessive reassurance to feel loved or secure
- Fearing being alone, even in unhealthy situations

For the anxiously attached individual, love often feels conditional. They have learned that closeness must be maintained through vigilance, caretaking, or emotional labor. Their nervous system responds to disconnection with panic. When the avoidant partner distances, the anxious person may escalate, plead, or cling—all in an effort to re-establish safety.

Distancing and the Avoidant Partner
The avoidant partner, equally shaped by their early experiences, copes with emotional intensity by retreating into independence. In the face of relational demands, their instinct is to create space. Distancing behaviors may include:

- Avoiding deep emotional conversations
- Focusing on work, hobbies, or tasks as a form of escape
- Withdrawing during conflict without explanation
- Resisting labels or commitment in relationships
- Downplaying the importance of connection

To the avoidant individual, these strategies feel necessary. Closeness activates fear—not necessarily of the other person, but of losing autonomy or being engulfed by emotion. They are not trying to hurt their partner; they are trying to regulate their own system, which has learned that emotional detachment is safety.

The Pain of Misattunement
At the heart of the anxious-avoidant cycle is **misattunement**—a chronic mismatch in emotional needs and communication styles. Each partner speaks a different emotional language, and neither knows how to translate.

- When the anxious person asks, "Do you love me?" the avoidant hears, "You're failing me."
- When the avoidant asks for space, the anxious person hears, "You don't care about me."
- When the anxious partner expresses pain, the avoidant may become defensive or shut down.
- When the avoidant partner detaches, the anxious person may explode with emotion, further overwhelming the avoidant.

These misunderstandings are not signs of incompatibility—they are signs of unhealed wounds colliding. Without intervention, both partners become locked in reactive roles. The anxious partner becomes more emotional, more controlling, more fearful. The avoidant becomes colder, more distant, more dismissive. The emotional gap widens until connection feels impossible.

And yet, both partners often feel trapped—not because they don't care, but because they don't know how to stop the cycle. They want closeness but don't feel safe getting there. They want harmony but don't know how to de-escalate. They love each other but speak through fear.

The good news is that misattunement can be corrected. Co-dependency can be replaced with healthy interdependence. Emotional distance can be bridged with curiosity and compassion. But first, each partner must become aware of the role they play—and why they play it.

The following case study offers a real-life example of how these patterns unfold—and how they can be transformed.

Real-Life Case Study: Breaking the Cycle

Background:

A couple, whom we'll call Mara and Eli, entered therapy after six years together. They were considering ending their relationship. Their arguments had become frequent and circular. Mara described feeling "invisible" and "emotionally starved." Eli felt "pressured" and "constantly criticized." Despite their frustrations, both said they loved each other deeply and didn't want to lose what they had built.

Attachment Dynamics:

Mara had an anxious attachment style. She grew up with a mother who was affectionate at times but also critical and emotionally inconsistent. As a child, Mara learned to perform for love—being helpful, agreeable, and emotionally expressive in hopes of securing warmth. As an adult, she carried these behaviors into relationships. She often second-guessed her partner's affection, overanalyzed texts, and needed frequent reassurance.

Eli had an avoidant attachment style. Raised in a home where emotions were not openly discussed, he learned early to manage distress alone. His parents valued independence, and any expression of vulnerability was met with discomfort or dismissal. In adulthood, Eli avoided emotional conversations, minimized problems, and coped with stress by retreating into work or solitude.

The Cycle:

Their dynamic played out in predictable ways. When Mara felt disconnected, she would reach out—sending long messages, asking for more quality time, expressing her fears. Eli, overwhelmed by the emotional intensity, would pull away—becoming less responsive, avoiding conversations, or physically leaving the space. This would trigger Mara's anxiety, leading to even more protest behavior, which in turn deepened Eli's withdrawal.

Both felt unheard. Mara believed Eli didn't care. Eli believed Mara would never be satisfied. Both were partially right—and both were reacting from old wounds.

Therapeutic Breakthrough:

In therapy, the focus shifted from blaming each other to understanding each other. Through attachment education, Mara and Eli began to see the deeper patterns at play. Mara realized that her intensity wasn't inherently wrong—it was a response to feeling unsafe. But she also saw how her constant pursuit made Eli feel emotionally trapped. Eli began to recognize that his withdrawal, while self-soothing, communicated abandonment to Mara. He wasn't rejecting her—he was protecting himself. But in doing so, he reinforced her worst fear.

Together, they learned tools for **co-regulation**—the ability to stay emotionally present without escalating. Mara began practicing emotional containment—pausing before reaching out, soothing herself first, and expressing needs in a grounded tone. Eli practiced staying in conversations longer, naming his need for space *without* disappearing, and validating Mara's feelings instead of minimizing them.

They created a "reset routine" for conflict:

- Step 1: Pause when overwhelmed
- Step 2: Check in with their own emotions
- Step 3: Reconnect through a shared statement of intention, e.g., *"I want to stay close to you, even though I need space right now."*
- Step 4: Set a clear time to return to the conversation

Over time, their reactive cycle softened. Mara no longer chased reassurance with desperation. Eli no longer viewed emotional needs as threats. They both learned to speak from their wounds without acting from them.

Outcome:

Mara and Eli didn't become perfect partners. But they became conscious ones. They still had disagreements, but they no longer spiraled. Emotional safety became the new foundation of their relationship—not through force, but through mutual understanding, daily practice, and a shared commitment to healing.

Their story is not unique. It is the story of countless couples locked in attachment cycles. But it is also proof that those cycles can be broken. That intimacy can become safe. That fear can give way to trust.

Chapter 5: Emotional Dysregulation and Unhealed Patterns

How Attachment Wounds Disrupt Emotional Flow

Emotions, at their core, are not the problem. They are messengers—signals that tell us what we need, what we value, and where we hurt. In securely attached individuals, emotions rise, are expressed, and settle again. There is flow. There is space for the self and others. But for those with attachment wounds, emotional flow is not so simple. It is disrupted, blocked, or dysregulated. What should be a signal becomes a storm.

When emotional needs are invalidated in early childhood, the ability to process emotion in healthy, self-regulating ways is compromised. This is not because the individual is broken or incapable—it is because the emotional system was never properly supported in its development. The child may have been taught—directly or indirectly—that their feelings were wrong, shameful, inconvenient, or even dangerous. As a result, they grow up unsure of how to identify, express, or regulate what they feel.

In this disrupted system, two common outcomes emerge: emotional suppression (common in avoidant attachment) or emotional flooding (common in anxious attachment). Suppression leads to a narrowing of emotional experience—numbness, detachment, and internal rigidity. Flooding leads to amplification—intensity, volatility, and a sense of being overwhelmed by feelings. Both are forms of dysregulation, and both make connection with others more difficult.

Disruption also happens in the space between feeling and action. Those with unhealed attachment wounds often cannot pause between emotion and response. If they feel rejected, they lash out or shut down. If they feel afraid, they cling or flee. If they feel unseen, they withdraw into silence or erupt in protest. There is no internal buffer—only raw reactivity.

This leads to a host of problems in adult relationships. People with dysregulated emotional systems may:

- Struggle to stay calm during conflict
- Experience disproportionate emotional responses to small triggers
- Feel misunderstood or overreacted to by others
- Have difficulty naming their emotions in real time
- Feel embarrassed, guilty, or ashamed after expressing emotion
- Fear that their feelings make them "too much" or "not enough"

These are not signs of personal failure. They are symptoms of a nervous system that was never taught to self-soothe in the presence of safe connection. Many people with attachment wounds were left alone in their big feelings as children. They had to learn to either bottle them up or turn them up in hopes of being seen. Either way, the core issue remains: *emotional expression feels unsafe.*

Healing begins with recognizing that dysregulation is not your fault—but it is your responsibility. You didn't create the original wound, but you are now in a position to offer yourself the support that was missing. To do that, you must first become aware of the emotional survival strategies that have shaped your identity.

Recognizing Your Emotional Survival Strategies
Everyone has emotional strategies. These are the ways we protect ourselves from discomfort, pain, or perceived threat. In securely attached individuals, these strategies are adaptive and flexible. In those with insecure attachment, they tend to be rigid, unconscious, and tied to early survival patterns.

Emotional survival strategies are not the same as personality traits. They are coping mechanisms—rehearsed behaviors that once kept you emotionally safe in a difficult environment. The problem is that these strategies, while helpful in childhood, often become maladaptive in adulthood. What once protected you now blocks you.

Let's look at some common emotional survival strategies and how they manifest across attachment styles:

1. Hypervigilance (Anxious Attachment)

Hypervigilance is the constant scanning of others for signs of disconnection, rejection, or emotional shift. This strategy develops in environments where love was inconsistent—where safety depended on noticing the mood of a parent or caregiver and adjusting behavior accordingly.

In adulthood, this may show up as:

- Reading into texts, tone, or facial expressions

- Overanalyzing every word spoken in an argument
- Watching for signs your partner is losing interest
- Becoming consumed with proving your worth or being "good enough"

Hypervigilance keeps you externally focused and internally anxious. It can lead to emotional exhaustion and a diminished sense of self.

2. Detachment (Avoidant Attachment)

Detachment is the refusal—conscious or unconscious—to engage emotionally. It arises when emotional expression was punished or ignored in childhood. If vulnerability led to pain, the child learns to disconnect as a means of survival.

In adulthood, detachment looks like:

- Shutting down in arguments
- Dismissing your own emotions as "not a big deal"
- Avoiding intimacy even when you crave it
- Keeping relationships on the surface to prevent being overwhelmed

Detachment gives the illusion of control, but it often leads to isolation, misunderstanding, and emotional loneliness.

3. People-Pleasing (Anxious-Fused Strategy)

People-pleasing is a common adaptation in anxious types who learned that connection came at the cost of self-expression. If love was only given when you were agreeable, compliant, or helpful, you may have internalized a belief that your worth depends on your ability to meet others' needs.

This strategy may include:

- Saying yes when you want to say no
- Prioritizing others' feelings over your own
- Avoiding conflict at all costs
- Feeling guilty for having boundaries or needs

While people-pleasing may create short-term harmony, it erodes authenticity and leads to resentment and burnout.

4. Control and Overfunctioning

Control is often used to manage internal chaos. If you grew up in an unpredictable or emotionally unstable environment, you may have learned that control—over yourself, others, or outcomes—was the only way to feel safe.

As an adult, this can manifest as:

- Micromanaging your environment or relationships
- Planning excessively or avoiding spontaneity
- Becoming rigid in your routines or expectations
- Fixating on other people's behavior to manage your own anxiety

Control feels like safety, but it often masks a deep fear of emotional collapse.

Recognizing these strategies doesn't mean rejecting them. It means honoring them for what they once were—your best efforts to survive. But you are not a child anymore. You have more tools now. More choices. The goal is not to shame these strategies, but to gently update them. To replace reactivity with intention. To expand your capacity for emotional presence—especially in the moments when your old patterns are most activated.

And that requires understanding the physiological system that governs all of this: the nervous system.

The Nervous System's Role in Reactivity

Emotional dysregulation is not simply a psychological problem—it is a physiological one. The nervous system is the body's command center for safety. It governs how we respond to stress, how we interpret connection or threat, and how we regulate ourselves emotionally in the presence of others. For those with unhealed attachment wounds, this system is often dysregulated—stuck in patterns of hyperactivation or shutdown.

The **autonomic nervous system (ANS)** is responsible for our involuntary responses to stress. It has two primary branches: the **sympathetic nervous system (SNS)**, which activates the fight-or-flight response, and the **parasympathetic nervous system (PNS)**, which promotes rest and recovery. In healthy regulation, these systems work in balance. We respond to stress, recover, and return to equilibrium.

But when attachment wounds are present, the nervous system often becomes locked in one of two patterns:

- **Hyperarousal (anxious attachment):** The SNS is overactive. The body is constantly on alert, scanning for signs of abandonment or danger. The result is anxiety, racing thoughts, muscle tension, and emotional flooding.
- **Hypoarousal (avoidant attachment):** The PNS dominates in a dissociative or shutdown state. The body goes numb. Emotions are muted or inaccessible. There is a sense of disconnection, flatness, or emotional fatigue.

These patterns are not conscious choices—they are *neurological responses* developed in response to early emotional pain. When a person with insecure attachment is triggered, their nervous system reacts before their rational mind has a chance to intervene. That's why someone can go from calm to panicked in a single moment—or from connected to emotionally absent with no warning.

Understanding your nervous system is essential for healing attachment-related reactivity. Without this awareness, you may interpret your symptoms as personal failures. But when you realize your body is responding to past danger—not present threat—you can begin to intervene with compassion.

Tools for nervous system regulation include:

- **Grounding techniques** (such as naming five things you see, hear, and feel in the present moment)
- **Breathwork** (especially slow, deep exhalations to activate the calming branch of the PNS)

- **Movement** (such as walking, stretching, or shaking to discharge activation)
- **Co-regulation** (seeking safe, supportive presence from another person to stabilize your nervous system)
- **Somatic tracking** (noticing sensations in the body without judgment to build awareness and tolerance)

These practices do not bypass emotional work—they support it. They create the physiological conditions for emotional repair. When your body feels safe, your mind can stay open. When your nervous system is regulated, you don't have to react—you can respond.

Over time, with practice, your nervous system becomes more flexible. You expand what is called your **"window of tolerance"**—the range of emotional experience you can handle without shutting down or becoming overwhelmed. This is the foundation of secure attachment. Not perfection, but presence. Not the absence of emotion, but the ability to stay with yourself in emotion.

As you develop this capacity, old patterns begin to lose their grip. You no longer spiral every time someone is late to respond. You no longer flee every time someone gets close. You begin to trust—not just others, but your own ability to stay emotionally safe in any circumstance.

This is not just psychological growth—it is *physiological transformation*. It is the rewiring of a system that once believed love was dangerous. And it is the beginning of a new way of being—grounded, attuned, and emotionally free.

Chapter 6: Self-Sabotage and Fear of Vulnerability

Walls Built by Avoidance, Cravings of the Anxious

Vulnerability should be the gateway to intimacy, but for those with insecure attachment, it often feels more like a trap. The idea of being emotionally seen, heard, and known—while deeply desired—can simultaneously evoke dread. This is the internal paradox of attachment wounds: a longing for closeness bound tightly with the terror of what closeness might expose.

At the core of insecure attachment lies a basic human need: to be accepted as we are, without fear of abandonment or enmeshment. However, when early relationships taught us that our feelings were dangerous, embarrassing, or unwelcome, we built internal defenses. These defenses now operate in our adult relationships as walls of protection—but they can also become prisons.

For avoidantly attached individuals, vulnerability is instinctively equated with weakness or threat. In childhood, emotional exposure may have led to rejection, ridicule, or indifference. The lesson internalized was: *If I show my feelings, I lose control—or worse, I lose love.* In response, avoidant types learn to suppress vulnerability, erecting emotional walls so no one can get close enough to hurt them. They may engage in distancing behaviors, deflection, or cynicism to avoid emotional intimacy. When a partner reaches for them emotionally, their reflex is to back away, change the subject, or intellectualize the interaction.

This isn't because avoidant individuals don't feel—they do. But their emotional reflex is wired to equate connection with danger, so they preserve the illusion of self-sufficiency instead. Unfortunately, the very walls built to protect them also shut out the nourishment they truly need: reciprocal love, empathy, and attuned presence.

On the other hand, anxiously attached individuals experience the vulnerability paradox in reverse. For them, emotional closeness is their deepest craving. They yearn to merge, to feel chosen, to be constantly reassured that they matter. But because they were often met with inconsistency in childhood, they also expect rejection. This creates a push-pull of its own: *I need you, but I'm afraid you'll leave. I want to open my heart, but I fear it will be crushed.*

Anxious individuals may over-disclose too early in relationships, use vulnerability as a way to test connection, or seek emotional intensity as proof of love. But beneath the surface, their sharing is often driven by fear, not grounded security. When that vulnerability isn't met in the way they hoped—or worse, is met with withdrawal—they spiral into self-doubt, shame, or emotional protest.

In both cases—avoidant or anxious—the core problem is the same: vulnerability was never modeled as safe. As a result, it becomes distorted. Avoidants protect themselves by suppressing it. Anxious individuals try to fast-track it. And both end up locked in self-sabotaging behaviors that prevent authentic connection.

Healing this pattern begins by recognizing how fear disguises itself in our behavior—and how we've unconsciously sabotaged the very love we long for.

How Fear Manifests as Control, Withdrawal, or Clinginess

Fear of vulnerability rarely announces itself directly. It doesn't say, "I'm afraid of being hurt." Instead, it arrives in disguise—through behaviors that feel self-protective but ultimately undermine trust and intimacy. Whether through control, withdrawal, or clinginess, the root cause is often the same: *I don't believe I'll be safe if I'm truly seen.*

Let's look at the most common expressions of this fear and how they function in real-life relationships.

1. Control: The Illusion of Safety

Control is often a subtle form of self-sabotage. When people feel emotionally unsafe, they attempt to manage their environment, their partner's behavior, or their own internal experience through control. This might look like:

- Needing constant updates from a partner (Where are you? Who are you with?)
- Managing every detail of plans or communication to avoid uncertainty
- Becoming overly focused on fixing or rescuing others
- Trying to influence or regulate how others respond emotionally

At the heart of control is the fear of emotional chaos. If things feel uncertain, the nervous system interprets it as a threat. So control becomes the strategy—*If I can predict, manage, or fix everything, I won't be blindsided or abandoned.*

But control erodes trust. It tells the other person, "I don't trust you to meet my needs unless I manage you." Over time, it creates resentment, distance, or emotional compliance—all of which damage intimacy.

2. Withdrawal: The Protective Retreat

Withdrawal is the hallmark of avoidant attachment, but it's also a universal response to emotional overwhelm. When feelings become too intense, or when the fear of exposure is activated, many people shut down. This might show up as:

- Stonewalling during arguments
- Avoiding conflict altogether
- Going silent after emotional intimacy
- Physically leaving a situation without explanation
- Emotional flatness or numbness

Withdrawal provides temporary relief from emotional discomfort. It creates space. But it also creates ambiguity. The partner left behind often feels abandoned or confused, triggering their own attachment insecurities. This can set off a destructive cycle: one partner withdraws, the other pursues, both become more dysregulated.

For the withdrawer, the key is to recognize when retreat becomes avoidance. Are you taking time to regulate—or to avoid feeling? Are you stepping back to breathe—or shutting down to suppress? Learning to stay emotionally present—without becoming overwhelmed—is a core task in healing.

3. Clinginess: The Compulsion to Merge

Clinginess is often misunderstood. It isn't about weakness—it's about unresolved fear. For anxiously attached individuals, the fear of being alone can feel existential. Emotional distance activates panic: *If they pull away, I'll be abandoned. If I'm not close, I'll be forgotten.*

Clinginess may look like:

- Excessive texting or calling
- Needing constant affirmation of love or commitment
- Becoming distressed by small changes in behavior
- Pushing for faster emotional intimacy
- Struggling to tolerate a partner's need for space

This behavior is not manipulative—it's adaptive. It's the anxious brain trying to regain a sense of safety. But when expressed unconsciously, it often overwhelms partners and reinforces the fear it's meant to soothe. The partner pulls away, the anxious person clings harder, and the cycle continues.

What's needed here is not less feeling—but more regulation. When anxiously attached individuals learn to self-soothe, their need for external reassurance softens. They can then express their needs with clarity rather than panic, and that changes everything.

In all three patterns—control, withdrawal, and clinginess—the underlying fear is the same: *If I show my true self, I'll be rejected, abandoned, or consumed.* These patterns are survival strategies. But they come at a cost. The cost is emotional connection. The cost is intimacy.

Recognizing these patterns is not about blame—it's about reclaiming your power. Once you see your protective behaviors for what they are, you can begin to choose differently. You can soften control into trust. Transform withdrawal into presence. Alchemize clinginess into confident connection.

And in doing so, you'll begin to dismantle the dysfunctional norms that once defined your version of love.

When Love Hurts: Recognizing Dysfunctional Norms

For many people with insecure attachment, pain in relationships feels normal. Chaos is familiar. Anxiety is expected. Love has been entangled with fear for so long that calm connection feels boring—or even suspicious. This is what happens when dysfunctional relational patterns become internalized as truth.

You may find yourself thinking:

- "If they don't make me anxious, I must not really love them."
- "If I'm not constantly working for their attention, it must not be real."
- "If I feel safe, I'll let my guard down and get hurt."

- "They're too nice. Something must be wrong with them."
- "It's better not to need anyone. Then I can't be disappointed."

These thoughts are not truths—they are trauma echoes. They reflect relational conditioning that taught you love must be earned, trust is dangerous, and closeness equals pain. But they can feel so familiar, so "true," that anything different feels threatening or alien.

Many people with insecure attachment unconsciously replicate the emotional dynamics of their childhood. If love was inconsistent, they seek partners who are emotionally unavailable. If love was suffocating, they pursue relationships with rigid boundaries. Even when these patterns are painful, they feel *predictable*. And the nervous system loves predictability—even when it hurts.

The result is self-sabotage. When someone safe, present, and available enters your life, you may reject them. Not because you don't care—but because they don't fit the blueprint. Your system isn't calibrated to trust steadiness. It's calibrated to expect disruption.

Breaking this pattern requires a radical shift in what you accept as normal.

Healthy Love Is Not Intense Chaos
It is calm. Respectful. Grounded. It does not create anxiety. It does not trigger abandonment wounds daily. It does not require you to shrink, perform, or guess.

Healthy love allows for:

- Emotional consistency
- Direct communication
- Space without punishment
- Boundaries without fear
- Needs without shame
- Disagreements without destruction

If that kind of love feels "boring" or "too easy," it's a sign that your nervous system has been shaped by dysfunctional norms. The path to healing involves **retraining your emotional responses**—learning that peace is not a danger, that you can be seen without being hurt, and that you are allowed to feel safe.

This doesn't happen overnight. It happens slowly, through small acts of courage: staying present when you want to flee, expressing a need without apology, letting someone care for you without earning it.

It also happens through grief—grieving the love you didn't get, the protection you didn't have, and the patterns you once believed were your fault. This grief is not weakness—it is the soil of growth.

When you begin to recognize your dysfunctional norms, you reclaim your right to something better. You no longer have to settle for chaos disguised as passion. You no longer have to lose yourself to keep someone else. You no longer have to live in fear that love will destroy you.

Instead, you can begin to build something new—something rooted in trust, mutual respect, and emotional integrity. Not perfect love. But safe, evolving, human love.

PART III: REPAIR BEGINS WITHIN — THE INNER WORK

Chapter 7: Awareness Is the First Repair Tool

Identifying Your Attachment Triggers

Awareness is the moment everything begins to change. Before behavior can shift, before emotional patterns can be rewired, before healing can root itself deeply—there must be a pause, a noticing, a name. You cannot heal what you cannot see. And in the realm of attachment, what often remains unseen are your *triggers*—those small, subtle cues that activate your nervous system and set your relational patterns into motion.

Attachment triggers are specific emotional stimuli—words, gestures, tones, actions—that signal to your body that connection is in jeopardy. They are the spark that lights the fuse. Sometimes obvious, sometimes hidden, these moments bring a sudden rush of feeling: anxiety, withdrawal, panic, shame. You may not know why you're upset, only that you suddenly *are*.

For the anxiously attached person, triggers often revolve around signs of perceived rejection, abandonment, or emotional distance. These may include:

- A delayed response to a text or call
- A partner seeming distracted, tired, or emotionally unavailable
- Changes in routine or affection
- Silence after conflict
- A shift in tone, expression, or eye contact

For the avoidantly attached person, triggers tend to be associated with closeness, pressure, or emotional exposure. Examples might include:

- Being asked to talk about feelings
- A partner expressing distress or need
- Feeling obligated to respond immediately
- Emotional intensity in conversation
- Feeling "cornered" or unable to leave a situation

These triggers aren't necessarily about what's happening in the present. They're about what happened in the *past*—and how your body remembers it. The nervous system doesn't operate on logic. It responds to familiarity. If closeness once meant engulfment, it will still feel threatening. If silence once meant rejection, it will still feel unbearable.

To begin the healing process, you must learn to *catch the moment of activation*. This is the split second between stimulus and reaction—when you feel the familiar surge, the old narrative beginning to speak. It is here, in this space, that transformation begins.

Ask yourself:

- What events or interactions consistently activate strong emotional reactions in me?

- Do I tend to get anxious or detached during certain relational experiences?

- What thoughts typically accompany these moments—what story am I telling myself?

- How does my body respond—tight chest, racing heart, numbness, stomach tension?

Start keeping a trigger journal. Not to judge yourself, but to observe with curiosity. Each entry is a clue—a pathway into the blueprint your attachment system has created. Over time, patterns will emerge. And with those patterns comes power. Because once you see the script, you can begin to *rewrite it*.

Rewriting Inner Scripts and Core Beliefs

Beneath every attachment response is a story. A script written long ago that still runs, unquestioned, through your mind and body. These scripts shape your identity, your relationships, and your emotional world. They are not facts—but they feel like the truth.

For the anxiously attached person, the script might say:

- "I must earn love to deserve it."

- "If I'm not needed, I'll be left."

- "I am too much."

- "People always leave when I get close."

- "I have to fix everything to stay connected."

For the avoidantly attached person, the script might sound like:

- "I can only trust myself."
- "If I open up, I'll lose control."
- "Needing someone is weakness."
- "People are unreliable."
- "If I depend on others, I'll be disappointed."

These are *core beliefs*—deep, emotionally encoded convictions that govern your thoughts, behaviors, and nervous system responses. They are not merely intellectual. They live in the body. They shape your tone, posture, eye contact, decision-making, and sense of safety.

To rewrite these scripts, you must first recognize them. Ask:

- What am I believing about myself when I'm triggered?
- What do I believe others think of me in moments of conflict or closeness?
- Where did I first learn this message—and from whom?
- Is this belief serving me now? Or is it keeping me stuck?

Awareness allows you to separate the *event* from the *interpretation*. Your partner being quiet doesn't *mean* they're leaving. Asking for space doesn't *mean* they're punishing you. Your emotion is valid—but the story may be outdated.

Begin practicing *thought reframing*—the act of challenging and replacing these beliefs with more compassionate, secure truths.

For example:

- From "I'm too needy" → to "My need for closeness is valid and human."

- From "I always get abandoned" → to "Some people have left, but others have stayed—and I am still here."

- From "I can't trust anyone" → to "Not everyone is safe, but I can learn to discern who is."

This is not toxic positivity. It's nervous-system re-education. It's giving your body new evidence, over time, that you are not in danger—that love can be safe, boundaries can be respected, and you do not have to perform or disappear to be loved.

It helps to pair thought reframing with *embodied practices*. Write the new belief. Speak it aloud. Pair it with breathwork. Feel the difference in your body when you say:

- "I am allowed to take up space."

- "I can be loved *as I am*."
- "I am safe even when someone is upset."

The more you repeat these new truths, especially during or after a triggering moment, the more your brain and body begin to believe them. Slowly, the script shifts. Your reactions soften. Your relationships change—not because others change, but because your internal framework has been rebuilt.

And at the heart of that rebuilding is the creation of *emotional safety within yourself*.

Creating Emotional Safety Within Yourself

Perhaps the most profound shift in attachment healing comes when you stop outsourcing your emotional safety. When you stop waiting for others to calm you, validate you, or make you feel worthy—and instead begin offering those things to yourself. This is the foundation of secure attachment: not the absence of need, but the presence of internal safety.

Emotional safety within yourself means that you become a stable, soothing presence for your own nervous system. You know how to respond to your emotions with compassion, not panic. You know how to hold space for your fear without abandoning yourself. You trust that you can survive the waves of emotion without drowning.

To create this inner safety, several practices are essential:

1. Develop Self-Compassionate Language

The way you speak to yourself in moments of distress determines whether you escalate or soothe your nervous system. Begin replacing critical self-talk with gentle, understanding words. Practice saying:

- "It makes sense that I feel this way."
- "This is an old wound being touched—I'm safe now."
- "I can breathe through this. I'm here with me."

You do not need to talk yourself *out* of your feelings. You need to remind yourself that feeling them doesn't mean you're unsafe or unworthy.

2. Build a "Safety Toolkit"

This is a collection of resources and practices that help you regulate during emotionally intense moments. Your toolkit might include:

- Grounding exercises (e.g., 5-4-3-2-1 technique)
- Breathwork (especially long exhalations)
- Journaling prompts to process emotion
- A calming phrase or mantra
- Music, movement, or sensory items that bring comfort

The goal isn't to avoid emotion—it's to *stay present* with it. To build capacity to feel, without reacting in self-destructive ways.

3. Reconnect With Your Body

Emotional safety is not just mental—it's physical. Many attachment wounds live in the body as tension, numbness, or hyperactivation. Begin developing a daily practice of checking in with your body:

- What sensations are present right now?
- Where do I feel tightness, heaviness, or lightness?
- Can I breathe into that space with compassion?

Somatic awareness helps you stay anchored in the present, reducing the chance of spiraling into old patterns.

4. Practice Boundaries and Emotional Containment

Creating inner safety also means learning to set boundaries—first with yourself. This means not letting your fear dictate your behavior. It means pausing before reacting. It means choosing not to send that fifth text, not because you don't care, but because you're learning to care *for yourself*.

It also means recognizing when your emotions are valid—but not your partner's responsibility to fix. You can say, "I'm feeling anxious right now," without expecting the other person to make it go away. This is *emotional containment*—the ability to hold your own emotional experience without needing someone else to carry it for you.

Over time, these practices create a powerful internal shift. You begin to trust *yourself*. You know that whatever happens—whether someone pulls away, whether conflict arises, whether fear returns—you can stay grounded. You can stay whole. You can stay loving.

This does not mean you don't need others. It means you no longer need them to *stabilize* you. You begin to engage from a place of choice, not compulsion. From presence, not protection.

And that, more than any technique or theory, is what heals attachment.

Chapter 8: Emotional Rewiring Through Mindfulness and Somatic Tools

The Body's Memory of Attachment Trauma

Trauma is not just something that happened in the past—it is something that continues to live in the body. For those with insecure attachment, early emotional wounds are not only stored in the mind but imprinted in the nervous system. The body holds a record of every moment closeness felt dangerous, every time vulnerability was punished, and every instance when comfort was absent. This record is not remembered through words or images, but through sensations, reactions, and instinctive responses.

Attachment trauma often begins long before conscious memory. An infant who cries and is not soothed learns that expressing distress leads to more discomfort, not less. A child whose emotions are invalidated or ridiculed learns to mute their internal world. Over time, these experiences become embedded not just in thought, but in *felt sense*. The result is a body that reacts to connection as if it were a threat—even when no danger is present.

You may notice this in yourself in subtle ways:

- A tight chest when someone gets emotionally close

- A racing heart when a partner pulls away

- A stomach drop when someone expresses dissatisfaction

- A frozen feeling during conflict

- A sense of numbness in moments when emotion should be accessible

These are not random. They are physiological expressions of emotional memory. The body has learned to protect you by preparing for pain. It readies you for fight, flight, freeze, or fawn—not because it's misfiring, but because it remembers.

This is why traditional cognitive approaches to attachment healing—such as affirmations or logic-based thinking—often fall short. You can tell yourself that you're safe, that your partner cares, that love is stable, but if your body still believes otherwise, the fear persists. The mind says yes. The body says no.

Healing must therefore include the body. Emotional rewiring requires engaging with the nervous system directly—through practices that bring awareness to sensation, regulate physiological arousal, and slowly recondition your internal responses to closeness, vulnerability, and presence.

This is where **mindfulness** and **somatic tools** come in. These approaches help you access the part of your experience that lives beneath words—your breath, your posture, your tension, your stillness. They invite you to create safety from the inside out—not by overriding your body, but by befriending it.

As you move through these practices, the goal is not to eliminate emotion. It's to expand your capacity to *feel* without becoming overwhelmed, to stay present in moments when you would once shut down or erupt. Over time, this builds emotional flexibility—what psychologists call an "increased window of tolerance."

You begin to shift from survival mode to regulation. From reaction to response. From avoidance or anxiety to secure presence.

Grounding, Breathing, and Reassociating Safety
To begin healing attachment wounds through the body, you must first create a sense of safety in the present moment. This is called **grounding**—the practice of anchoring your awareness in the here and now, so that past emotions and future fears lose their grip on your nervous system.

Grounding is essential because attachment trauma often pulls you out of the present. When a partner pulls away, you don't just feel their absence—you feel every abandonment that came before. When someone expresses anger, you don't just hear their frustration—you hear every voice that once criticized or shamed you. Grounding helps bring you back to now. To remind your body: *This is not then. This is not the same.*

Here are foundational grounding and breathwork tools that form the heart of emotional rewiring:

1. Grounding Techniques

These tools help reestablish a connection between your mind and body. They are especially useful when you feel overwhelmed, dissociated, anxious, or emotionally flooded.

The 5-4-3-2-1 Technique (Sensory Grounding):

- **5 things you see**
- **4 things you can touch**
- **3 things you hear**
- **2 things you smell**
- **1 thing you taste**

This exercise pulls your awareness into the physical environment. It reorients your nervous system to the external world, signaling that you are safe in this moment.

Feet-on-the-Floor Grounding:

- Sit or stand still. Place your feet flat on the ground.
- Push gently into the floor and notice the sensation.
- Feel the weight of your body being supported.
- Repeat: *"I am grounded. I am safe. I am here."*

These practices counteract dissociation and help interrupt reactive spirals before they take over.

2. Breathwork for Regulation

Breathing is the fastest way to influence your nervous system. When you are activated—either in anxious hyperarousal or avoidant shutdown—conscious breath can gently bring you back to balance.

The 4-7-8 Breath (Calming Breath):

- Inhale through your nose for 4 seconds
- Hold for 7 seconds
- Exhale slowly through your mouth for 8 seconds
- Repeat for 3–5 cycles

This breath pattern stimulates the parasympathetic nervous system (rest and digest), reducing heart rate and signaling to your body that it's safe to relax.

Box Breathing (Balancing Breath):

- Inhale for 4 seconds
- Hold for 4 seconds
- Exhale for 4 seconds
- Hold for 4 seconds
- Repeat in a steady rhythm

Box breathing helps you return to center when you're feeling emotionally overwhelmed but still need to stay alert and engaged.

3. Reassociating Safety With the Body

One of the core tasks in somatic healing is *reassociating* positive, safe experiences with your body—especially if touch, closeness, or intimacy were previously associated with fear. This can be done gently through:

- **Self-touch practices** (e.g., placing a hand on your heart, stroking your arms)

- **Safe eye contact with a trusted person**

- **Slow movement** (such as yoga, tai chi, or mindful walking)

- **Weighted blankets, warmth, or other comforting sensations**

As you engage with these tools, remind yourself: *My body is not my enemy. It has protected me. And now it is safe to soften.*

You do not have to force relaxation. You only need to stay present long enough for your body to learn that presence is safe.

These practices work best when repeated consistently—not just in moments of crisis, but as part of a daily rhythm. The more you condition your body to associate calm, connection, and emotional presence with safety, the more natural these states become.

And as your body softens, your mind becomes more receptive. That is where integration begins.

Integrating Cognitive and Somatic Awareness

Healing insecure attachment requires a bridge—a way to connect the insights of the mind with the instincts of the body. Left alone, cognitive awareness can become analysis without action. Somatic awareness can become sensation without understanding. But when the two work together, true transformation unfolds.

Integration means aligning what you know intellectually with what you feel physically. It's the process of helping your nervous system *believe* what your mind already understands.

For example:

- You *know* not every disagreement means rejection. But your heart still races, and your body braces as if it does.

- You *know* it's okay to ask for space. But when someone does, you still panic or protest.

This gap between knowledge and embodiment is where many people get stuck. They believe they're failing because their reactions persist, even after months of therapy or reflection. But it's not failure—it's physiology. The emotional brain needs new experiences, not just new thoughts.

Here's how to bridge that gap:

1. Pair New Beliefs With New Body States

When practicing reframed thoughts (e.g., *"I am safe to express emotion"*), do so while in a regulated state. Say it during breathwork. Write it after grounding. Repeat it while placing a hand on your chest.

This conditions your nervous system to associate the belief with safety. Over time, the emotional brain begins to *believe* what the thinking brain is saying.

2. Track Your Body in Triggering Moments

When activated, pause and ask:

- Where do I feel this in my body?
- Is it tight, hot, cold, numb, heavy?
- Can I stay with the sensation without reacting?

This builds tolerance for discomfort. It creates space between feeling and action. That space is where new choices are born.

3. Practice "Micro-Moments" of Safe Vulnerability

Rather than diving into intense emotional exposure, try small, safe acts of openness:

- Sharing a feeling with someone you trust
- Asking for support in a low-stakes situation
- Saying "I feel anxious" instead of acting on it

After each moment, reflect on how your body responded. Offer it reassurance. *"That was brave. And I'm okay."*

These micro-moments build confidence. They expand your capacity for connection.

4. Return to the Body After Emotional Work

After a therapy session, conflict, or deep inner work, don't immediately distract or analyze. Instead, give your body time to integrate:

- Lie down and place a weighted object on your chest
- Take a walk and feel your feet on the earth
- Do gentle stretching or self-massage
- Rest in silence

This completes the loop. It helps your system process—not just intellectually, but experientially.

Integration is not a one-time event. It is a practice. A way of living that honors both your thoughts *and* your sensations. It is what allows insight to become embodiment. And embodiment is what creates secure attachment—not as an abstract idea, but as a lived, felt truth.

Chapter 9: Building Secure Internal Attachment

Reparenting the Inner Child

Behind every attachment wound is a child who needed something they didn't receive—emotional consistency, safety, validation, affection, attunement. When those needs went unmet, the child didn't just experience momentary sadness. They internalized a story: *I am not safe to feel. I am too much. I must manage this alone.*

That child doesn't disappear. They live on inside the adult body, still reacting to the world with the same fear and longing. They cry silently when a partner pulls away. They panic when love feels uncertain. They shut down when asked to express what they feel. This isn't immaturity—it's unhealed pain.

To build secure internal attachment, you must re-establish a connection with this part of yourself—the vulnerable, emotionally honest, often hidden inner child. This is the part of you that holds the original blueprint for connection. Reparenting is not about indulging immaturity. It's about restoring the emotional relationship between the wise adult self and the wounded child self. It's about becoming the caregiver you never had.

The first step in reparenting is **acknowledgment**. Begin by recognizing when your inner child is active. Often, they show up in the following ways:

- You feel emotionally overwhelmed and helpless

- You react impulsively or with disproportionate fear

- You crave validation or panic at the thought of abandonment

- You freeze in conflict or feel incapable of expressing needs

- You experience shame after vulnerability

When you feel these sensations arise, pause and ask, *Who is reacting right now—my adult self or a younger part of me?* This question alone creates a bridge between your emotional past and your present self-awareness.

Next is **dialogue**. Speak gently to the inner child as you would to someone small and scared. You might say:

- "I see you. You're safe now."

- "You're not alone anymore. I'm here."

- "It's okay to feel this. I won't abandon you."

- "You didn't cause this. You're not too much."

You can journal from both voices: let the child speak their fears, and let the adult respond with compassion and steadiness. Over time, this internal relationship becomes more natural, more secure. The child learns they no longer have to act out or shut down to be heard.

Daily rituals can also help this bond form. You might:

- Visualize holding your inner child each morning
- Write letters to them in your journal
- Keep a childhood photo nearby as a reminder of your commitment
- Offer comfort through calming actions—soft music, warm blankets, gentle movement

Reparenting is a practice of showing up. Not to fix or silence, but to *listen*. To build trust slowly, through repeated moments of compassion.

And like all relationships, it deepens with time. Your inner child begins to trust your presence. Your adult self becomes less reactive, more stable. This is what secure internal attachment feels like: a steady connection with yourself, even in the face of fear.

But self-connection alone isn't enough. To truly build secure attachment, you must also develop the emotional muscles of compassion and containment—the tools that keep your inner world safe, no matter what is happening externally.

Cultivating Self-Compassion and Emotional Containment

When your early environment lacked emotional support, you likely developed a harsh internal voice. This voice judges your reactions, minimizes your needs, and criticizes your pain. It echoes caregivers who dismissed your feelings or expected you to "get over it" quickly. Over time, this voice becomes internalized as a protector—but it rarely protects. More often, it deepens the wound.

Cultivating self-compassion is about softening that voice—not by silencing it, but by introducing a new one. A voice that says, *You make sense. You're doing your best. You deserve kindness.* This is not self-pity. It is the necessary antidote to shame.

Self-compassion includes three core components:

1. **Mindful awareness of suffering**: Noticing when you are in emotional pain, without minimizing or ignoring it.

2. **Recognition of common humanity**: Remembering that your struggles are part of being human. You are not defective or alone.

3. **Kind self-talk**: Responding to yourself as you would to a loved one in pain—with patience, gentleness, and affirmation.

Practicing self-compassion may feel foreign at first. Especially for those with avoidant patterns, offering softness inward can trigger discomfort. For those with anxious patterns, self-compassion may feel insufficient—they still crave external reassurance. But the more you practice, the more your nervous system begins to recognize this new tone as safe.

You might start with a daily affirmation:

- "Today, I give myself grace."

- "I am worthy of care, especially from myself."
- "I can be gentle with my fear."
- "Even when I struggle, I am still whole."

Pair these phrases with breath, with self-touch, or with moments of pause. Let them settle into your body.

Alongside compassion, you must also build **emotional containment**—the ability to hold emotional experience without becoming overwhelmed by it or projecting it outward destructively. Containment is the internal container where emotions can rise, exist, and pass without needing to be acted upon. It is not suppression—it is stewardship.

Containment looks like:

- Feeling sadness without spiraling into despair
- Noticing anger without exploding or shutting down
- Holding fear without begging for instant reassurance
- Being able to say, "I'm triggered, and I can sit with this"
- Delaying reaction long enough to respond from intention, not fear

This is the emotional maturity that secure attachment requires. It does not mean you don't feel deeply—it means you know how to hold your feelings with care.

A useful metaphor is that of being your own "emotional parent." When a child is upset, they don't need their feelings fixed—they need to know that someone is calm, steady, and not afraid of their distress. You can become that presence for yourself. You can say:

- "This is hard. And I can handle it."

- "My emotions are not dangerous—they are signals."

- "I can ride this wave without letting it crash me."

As you grow in compassion and containment, your relational patterns begin to shift. You no longer need others to rescue you or stay away. You become the stable center of your own experience. You become safe—for yourself, and eventually, for others.

This is how you build a secure internal foundation. But to truly embody secure attachment, you must take one more step: becoming the *secure base* you never had.

Becoming the Secure Base You Never Had
The term "secure base" comes from attachment theory and refers to a caregiver who provides both a safe haven and a launching pad. This person is consistent, responsive, and emotionally available. When present, they allow the child to explore the world, knowing they can always return for comfort and safety.

For many, that secure base never existed. Or if it did, it was inconsistent or conditional. As adults, the absence of this foundation shows up as insecurity, dependency, fear of abandonment, or emotional detachment. Without a secure base, you may find it hard to rest, to trust, to take risks, or to let love in.

Becoming your own secure base means you create that safety internally. You develop the ability to both soothe yourself and encourage growth. You become the voice that says:

- "You can try new things, and I'll be here if it's hard."

- "You're safe to rest. You're not falling apart."

- "You don't need to earn love or approval. You already have it."

- "You can feel this. You're not alone."

This is the balance of **self-nurture and self-leadership**. You comfort the parts of you that are scared, *and* you challenge the parts of you that want to stay stuck. You offer compassion *and* accountability. Love *and* boundaries.

Becoming a secure base also means developing **emotional trust in yourself**. You begin to trust:

- That your feelings are valid

- That you can handle relational ups and downs

- That you can discern safe people from unsafe ones

- That you can express yourself without fear of rejection

- That you don't have to abandon yourself to stay connected

As this trust grows, everything changes. You stop needing others to regulate you. You stop chasing or withdrawing reflexively. You begin to show up authentically—not perfectly, but consistently. You communicate your needs with clarity. You allow space for others to do the same. You welcome intimacy—not because you're unafraid, but because you know how to stay anchored.

This inner security becomes visible. Others feel it. Your relationships begin to reflect it. And over time, what once felt impossible—emotional closeness, safe vulnerability, balanced autonomy—becomes your new normal.

You are not the child who was neglected.
You are not the teenager who was ridiculed.
You are not the adult who had to pretend everything was fine.

You are the one who sees all of those selves. Who loves them. Who leads them forward.

You are your own secure base now.

And from this place, you can begin to engage with others—not from fear or longing, but from wholeness.

PART IV: HEALING IN RELATIONSHIP CONTEXTS

Chapter 10: Communicating Needs Without Anxiety or Withdrawal

How to Express Without Over-Explaining or Shutting Down

Communicating needs may sound simple, but for those with insecure attachment, it often feels like an emotional minefield. For the anxiously attached, asking for what they need can be tangled with shame, fear of rejection, or the compulsive urge to explain themselves endlessly. For the avoidantly attached, the struggle is often the opposite—they don't speak at all, withdrawing inward rather than risk vulnerability.

In both cases, the message becomes distorted. What starts as a need turns into either a plea or a shutdown. Neither brings connection. Both leave the individual feeling unseen, unmet, and misunderstood.

The problem isn't the need. It's how the need is communicated—or avoided.

Let's start with the **anxious communicator**. Often, when they feel a shift in connection—less affection, a slow reply, an unusual tone—they feel an urgent need to restore emotional closeness. But rather than express this directly, they may over-explain, repeat themselves, become overly apologetic, or spiral into panic. Their message might sound like:

- "I know this is silly, but I just need to know we're okay."

- "Maybe I'm being too much, but when you didn't text back, I got really anxious."

- "I'm sorry I'm so needy. I just can't help it."

While these statements are attempts to self-regulate through connection, they often result in emotional fatigue—for both the speaker and the listener. The core need—*to feel safe, reassured, and emotionally attuned to*—gets buried under layers of justification, self-doubt, and emotional urgency.

For the **avoidant communicator**, the impulse is to do the opposite. They feel discomfort rising and instinctively shut it down. Rather than speak, they internalize. They rationalize. They avoid it. Their silence is not indifference—it's fear. Fear that opening up will lead to being misunderstood, criticized, or overwhelmed.

Their internal dialogue might sound like:

- *"It's not a big deal. I'll just handle it."*

- *"Talking wont help. It'll just make things worse."*

- *"I don't even know what I'm feeling, so why bother saying anything?"*

In relationships, this looks like emotional shutdown, conflict avoidance, or sudden disappearance. Partners are often left guessing, hurt, or feeling shut out.

The antidote to both patterns begins with recognizing that needs are not weaknesses—they are relational information. You're not broken for having them. The question isn't *whether* you have needs, but *how* you share them.

Here are some foundational principles for expressing needs without over-explaining or withdrawing:

1. Lead With Clarity, Not Apology

Instead of saying, "I know this is silly, but..." say, "I'm noticing I feel anxious, and I'd like to check in." This frames your need as valid and invites connection without guilt.

2. Use Ownership Language

Say, "I feel [emotion] when [situation], and I need [need]."
  Example: "I feel distant when we go all day without speaking. I need a moment of connection to feel grounded."

3. Practice "One Breath" Delivery

Keep the request short and clear enough to be spoken in one breath. If you need to say more, wait until your partner responds.

4. Pause Before You Speak

Ask yourself, "What am I feeling? What do I actually need?" Then speak from that place, rather than from the impulse to defend, fix, or flee.

When you communicate from a regulated place, your words carry confidence rather than anxiety. You become easier to hear, and others are more likely to respond with presence rather than defensiveness.

You don't need a perfect script. You need presence, ownership, and the belief that your needs are worthy of being named.

Attachment-Informed Communication Techniques

Communicating from a secure place requires more than good intentions—it requires new tools. Attachment-informed communication acknowledges that behind every exchange is an emotional nervous system, shaped by past relationships and primed for threat or connection.

To speak and listen from an attachment-conscious perspective is to recognize that:

- People interpret tone and timing based on old wounds

- Emotional intensity often signals fear, not aggression

- Silence can mean overwhelm, not indifference
- Defensiveness is often a shield for shame

Below are key techniques to help you communicate in a way that invites safety, clarity, and closeness—whether you are anxiously or avoidantly wired.

1. Use the "When–I–Feel–I–Need" Formula

This simple but powerful structure helps you express your feelings without blame:

- **When** [this happens]
- **I feel** [this emotion]
- **I need** [this support or behavior]

Examples:

- "When we don't talk after an argument, I feel anxious. I need some kind of reconnection, even a brief check-in."
- "When I'm asked to talk before I'm ready, I feel pressured. I need time to process so I can respond clearly."

This method helps both anxious and avoidant individuals avoid mind reading, guilt-tripping, or shutting down.

2. Distinguish Feelings from Thoughts

Feelings are emotional states (*sad, hurt, anxious, overwhelmed*). Thoughts are interpretations (*you don't care, I'm being judged*). In communication, stay in the emotional lane. Instead of "You don't care about me," say "I feel disconnected and scared right now." This reduces defensiveness and encourages empathy.

3. Use "Soft Startups" in Conflict

Research shows that how a conversation begins strongly predicts how it ends. A soft startup is a way of initiating difficult conversations with calmness, care, and curiosity. For example:

- "Hey, I wanted to share something that's been on my mind. Is now a good time?"
- "I've been feeling a little off lately in our dynamic, and I'd love to talk through it."

Avoid blame, criticism, or demands. Start with emotional transparency and a collaborative tone.

4. Ask for Emotional Check-Ins

Especially in relationships with avoidant partners, regular emotional check-ins can create consistency without pressure. A simple weekly prompt like, "How are we feeling about our connection this week?" invites shared reflection and nurtures emotional safety.

5. Practice "Contain and Return"

If a conversation gets too heated or triggering, use this phrase:

- "Let's pause here. I want to stay connected, but I need a moment to regulate. Can we come back to this in 15 minutes?"

Contain the rupture. Then return to the conversation once both are grounded.

These techniques do more than just improve communication. They rewire your nervous system through relational safety. Every time you express a need without shame—or hear one without defensiveness—you update your internal model of connection.

You begin to learn: *It's safe to speak. It's safe to hear. It's safe to need.*

And with that foundation, repair becomes possible—even after conflict, misunderstanding, or misattunement.

Repairing Misattunement Through Active Listening
In every relationship, misattunement is inevitable. Even the most emotionally intelligent partners will miss cues, interpret things incorrectly, or become reactive. But what separates secure relationships from insecure ones is not the absence of misattunement—it's the presence of *repair*.

Repair is the act of reconnecting after a rupture. It is saying, "I see where I missed you," or "Let's try again." Repair transforms conflict into closeness and misunderstanding into mutual understanding.

And at the heart of repair is **active listening**—the skill of hearing someone not just to respond, but to understand.

Most of us believe we're good listeners. In reality, we're often waiting to defend, correct, or make a point. Especially when attachment wounds are activated, we listen through fear filters—*What are they really saying? Am I being rejected? Are they attacking me?*

To repair effectively, we must drop the agenda and attune instead.

The Core Skills of Active Listening
1. Presence
    Stop what you're doing. Put away distractions. Make eye contact if possible. Let your body language say: I'm here with you.

2. Reflection
    Repeat back the essence of what you heard, not verbatim, but emotionally.

- "It sounds like you felt hurt when I didn't respond to your message."

- "You're saying that when I pull away, it feels like I don't care. Is that right?"

3. Validation
   Affirm their emotional experience—even if you see it differently.

- "That makes sense. I can see how that would feel upsetting."
- "It's okay that you felt overwhelmed. I want to understand more."

4. Curiosity
   Ask questions that show interest, not interrogation.

- "What was that like for you?"
- "What do you need most when that happens?"

5. Accountability
   Own your part without defensiveness. Even if your intention was good, acknowledge the impact.

- "I didn't realize how that came across. I see it now."
- "That wasn't my intention, but I understand how it landed. I'm sorry."

Repair doesn't mean taking all the blame. It means creating a space where both people feel safe to be

honest—and committed to understanding each other better.
Active listening is especially healing in anxious-avoidant dynamics. When the avoidant partner learns to stay present, the anxious partner feels seen. When the anxious partner learns to express clearly, the avoidant feels less overwhelmed. Both begin to trust that conflict doesn't mean collapse. That closeness doesn't have to mean chaos.

The Power of Mutual Repair
In secure relationships, both partners take turns initiating repair. They don't wait to be right. They don't need the perfect words. They say:
- "Can we rewind? I think I missed you there."

- "That didn't come out right. Can I try again?"

- "I'm feeling defensive, but I want to stay connected."

These small gestures restore connection and rebuild trust. Over time, they change the emotional culture of the relationship. The atmosphere becomes one of safety, where missteps aren't fatal and expression isn't dangerous.
You learn that love can hold mistakes. That vulnerability doesn't have to lead to abandonment. That being human doesn't mean being unworthy.
This is the heart of attachment healing: not perfection, but repair. Not never falling, but learning how to reach for each other again.

Chapter 11: Setting Boundaries Without Shame or Guilt

Why Boundaries Are Essential for Safety and Respect

The word "boundary" often conjures images of walls, ultimatums, or pushing others away. But in reality, boundaries are not barriers—they are bridges. They create the structure within which intimacy can safely grow. Without them, relationships either become enmeshed and chaotic or distant and unsatisfying. With them, relationships are grounded, balanced, and built on mutual respect.

Boundaries are not about controlling others. They're about *clarifying yourself*—your limits, your values, your emotional bandwidth. They define where you end and where another person begins. They let others know how to love you well. More importantly, they teach *you* how to honor your needs without apology.

For those with insecure attachment, setting boundaries often feels dangerous. If your early relationships taught you that expressing needs leads to abandonment (anxious attachment) or that closeness erases autonomy (avoidant attachment), boundaries may feel like a risk. You might fear being rejected for asserting yourself or feel guilty for taking up emotional space.

But here's the truth: **boundaries are the foundation of safety in any connection.**

They:

- Protect your emotional well-being
- Prevent resentment and burnout
- Clarify expectations and reduce miscommunication
- Build trust—because others know where they stand with you
- Allow for authentic connection instead of performative closeness

In secure attachment, boundaries are *normal*. They are not punishments. They are signals: *This is what helps me stay present. This is what I need to remain open. This is how I stay connected to myself and others.*

For example:

- "I'm happy to talk, but I need a few minutes to regulate first."
- "I care about you, but I can't keep having this conversation late at night."
- "I want to support you, but I also need time to rest after work."
- "I'm okay with checking in, but not with tracking each other constantly."

These are not rejections. They're recalibrations. And when communicated with clarity and care, they often create deeper trust—not distance.

Boundaries also help prevent emotional entanglement. In anxious-avoidant dynamics, one partner may over-function while the other withdraws. Boundaries interrupt that pattern by encouraging both individuals to regulate themselves first. The anxious person learns to tolerate space. The avoidant person learns to remain engaged within safe limits. Both develop the muscle of emotional presence without sacrifice.

But in order to set boundaries that create connection rather than conflict, you must first know how to differentiate *avoidance* from *healthy limits*.

Differentiating Avoidance from Healthy Limits
Avoidance and boundaries can look similar on the surface. Both may involve stepping back, creating space, or saying no. But the energy behind them—and the emotional outcome—is very different.

Avoidance is fear-based. It seeks distance as protection. It often arises from discomfort with conflict, vulnerability, or emotional intimacy. Avoidance says:

- "If I withdraw, I won't get hurt."
- "If I don't talk about this, it'll go away."
- "If I stay quiet, they won't leave me."
- "If I keep it vague, I won't have to feel exposed."

Avoidance often leads to confusion in relationships. The other person senses disconnection but doesn't know why. There's silence, ambiguity, or passive behavior instead of directness. Over time, this erodes trust.

Boundaries, on the other hand, are clarity-based. They seek connection through honesty. They are rooted in self-awareness, not reactivity. Boundaries say:

- "I want to stay connected, and this is what I need to do that well."
- "I need a break—not because I don't care, but because I care about showing up calmly."
- "I can't say yes to this, but I can offer something else."
- "This is what works for me, and I'm open to hearing what works for you."

The difference lies in **intent and communication**. Avoidance hides. Boundaries communicate. Avoidance disconnects. Boundaries define.

To discern whether you're avoiding or setting a healthy boundary, ask yourself:

- Am I acting from fear or self-respect?
- Have I communicated my need clearly, or am I silently withdrawing?
- Does this decision create more clarity or more confusion?
- Am I open to connection after space, or am I trying to escape it entirely?

Healthy boundaries often feel *uncomfortable*, especially at first. If you were conditioned to ignore your needs or avoid upsetting others, even saying "no" can trigger guilt. But discomfort doesn't mean you're doing something wrong—it often means you're doing something *new*.

Avoidance feels like relief followed by disconnection. Boundaries feel like discomfort followed by clarity.

And once you learn how to set them up with love, they become acts of care—not just for yourself, but for your relationships as a whole.

Practicing Boundary-Setting With Love
Setting boundaries is not an act of aggression—it's an act of self-connection. But it must also be done relationally. Boundaries that are too rigid become walls. Boundaries that are too loose become invitations to repeat old patterns. The key is to **set limits that honor both your needs and your values**—with empathy, courage, and calm.

Here's how to practice loving, effective boundary-setting:

1. Clarify Your Boundary Before You Communicate It

Ask:

- What am I feeling?
- What am I needing?
- What behavior or pattern is not working for me?

- What would help me feel safe, respected, or balanced?

Example: You notice you feel drained after late-night conversations. Instead of blaming, clarify: *"I feel tired and anxious when I stay up too late talking. I need to limit emotional conversations to earlier hours."*

2. Use Direct, Compassionate Language

Boundaries are best received when stated simply and kindly. Avoid blame, assumptions, or excessive apology.

Instead of:

- "You always stress me out, and I can't deal with this anymore."
  Try:
- "I feel overwhelmed when we talk about heavy things late at night. I'd like to move those conversations to another time."

Instead of:

- "I'm sorry, I just can't do everything for you."
  Try:
- "I care about helping, and I need to protect my energy by limiting how often I check in."

3. Anticipate Discomfort—but Stay Grounded

When you set a new boundary, especially in a relationship where there's been enmeshment or poor communication, it may feel like you're doing something wrong. You might hear:

- "Why are you being distant?"
- "You've changed."
- "You're pushing me away."

Stay calm. Breathe. Remind yourself:

- *"This is new for them, but it's right for me."*
- *"I can be loving and firm at the same time."*
- *"Discomfort isn't danger—it's part of change."*

Boundaries often reveal relational patterns. They show you who can meet you in clarity—and who needs time or support to adjust.

4. Follow Through Gently but Consistently

A boundary only works if it's respected. That means not just setting it, but *holding it*—even when it's inconvenient. Follow-through builds self-trust.

If a partner repeatedly crosses a line you've expressed, you might say:

- "I've noticed this boundary isn't being honored. Can we talk about what's going on?"

- "I want to stay close, but I also need this limit to be respected so I feel safe."

Don't escalate. Don't withdraw. Stay relational. Stay clear.

5. Celebrate the Outcome

Each time you set a boundary with love, notice the impact on your nervous system. You may feel stronger, more grounded, more emotionally balanced. You may feel proud, even if others don't immediately understand.

This is how secure attachment grows—from the inside out. Not by people pleasing or stonewalling, but by showing up with honesty, care, and self-respect.

Over time, as you practice, boundary-setting becomes second nature. You stop fearing rejection or guilt. You start trusting your inner compass. You begin to choose relationships where boundaries are not punished—but welcomed.

Because healthy love doesn't demand self-abandonment. It celebrates mutual clarity.

Chapter 12: Rebuilding Intimacy and Trust

How to Tolerate Closeness Without Losing Yourself
For those shaped by insecure attachment, intimacy often feels like a contradiction. On one hand, there's a deep desire for connection—to be seen, understood, and loved. On the other, there's an equal fear of being consumed, rejected, or lost within that closeness. This push-pull of desire and defense creates an internal battle: *I want to let you in, but I don't know if it's safe.*

The reason for this paradox lies in the nervous system. If emotional closeness in early life was inconsistent, overwhelming, or conditional, the body remembers it not as comfort, but as confusion or chaos. In response, we develop adaptive strategies. We either lean in too far—merging with others to avoid abandonment—or pull away too soon, guarding against engulfment.

Tolerating closeness, then, isn't simply about opening up. It's about reconditioning the body and mind to experience intimacy as *safe*, *balanced*, and *mutually respectful*. It's about learning to stay connected to others *without disconnecting from yourself.*

This process starts with understanding the signs that your system is feeling threatened by closeness—even when you consciously desire it. These signs may include:

- Becoming overly agreeable or self-sacrificing

- Losing sight of your needs or boundaries in relationships
- Feeling anxious when someone pulls away or unavailable
- Feeling suffocated or irritable when someone gets too close
- Escalating or withdrawing after moments of vulnerability

Each of these responses is a cue: your attachment system has been activated. And rather than judge yourself for it, the healing response is to slow down and get curious.

Ask yourself:

- What do I fear will happen if I fully show up in this connection?
- When did I first learn that closeness was dangerous, conditional, or costly?
- How can I stay emotionally present without abandoning my own needs?

Start practicing **me-with-you** moments—times where you allow yourself to be connected while also anchored in self. For example:

- Sharing a feeling while also stating a need ("I'm feeling scared, and I need to take a break before we continue.")
- Checking in with your body during conversation ("Am I holding tension? Am I breathing?")

- Setting micro-boundaries ("I want to keep talking, but I'd like to sit on the couch instead of the bed.")

These small acts help you *retrain your nervous system* to recognize closeness as manageable—not overwhelming.

Equally important is learning that intimacy doesn't mean *access without limits*. You can say:

- "I love being close to you, and I also need space to process."
- "I want to share with you, but I need you to listen without trying to fix."
- "I can be emotionally available, and I still need alone time to recharge."

These statements affirm your right to stay emotionally sovereign, even in connection. They prevent enmeshment and reduce the fear that intimacy means self-erasure.

As you practice tolerating closeness, you build resilience. You stop viewing connection as something you must *survive* and begin experiencing it as something you can *enjoy*. You develop a new emotional template: *I can be close, and still be me.*

And in that space, real trust begins to grow.

Slowly Earning and Granting Trust

Trust is not something that happens all at once. It is earned in layers, over time, through consistent relational experiences. For those with attachment wounds, however, trust can feel like a fragile or dangerous endeavor—either withheld indefinitely or given too quickly out of desperation for connection.

To rebuild trust—whether with others or within yourself—you must learn the difference between blind trust and *earned trust*.

1. Blind Trust vs. Earned Trust

- **Blind trust** is given prematurely. It bypasses red flags, ignores intuition, and assumes that others will behave with integrity regardless of evidence. This often arises from anxious attachment, where the fear of abandonment overrides discernment.
- **Earned trust**, by contrast, is developed over time. It is based on observed behavior, emotional consistency, and mutual respect. It allows for boundaries, curiosity, and gradual deepening.

For the avoidant partner, learning to **grant trust** may involve letting go of the belief that people will inevitably disappoint, betray, or invade their space. It means allowing others to get close enough to prove their reliability—not once, but over time.

For the anxious partner, learning to **earn trust** means resisting the urge to rush intimacy or test connection through protest behaviors. It means tolerating space without assuming abandonment, and allowing trust to develop at a sustainable pace.

The path to earned trust includes the following principles:

2. Trust Is Built Through Consistency in Small Moments

We tend to think of trust as something decided in big events—crises, betrayals, declarations. But trust is built in the quiet, daily moments:

- When someone says they'll call and they do
- When a boundary is expressed and respected
- When a feeling is shared and received with care
- When a rupture happens and is repaired, not ignored

These moments create safety. They allow your nervous system to relax. And over time, they replace old scripts like "People always leave" or "No one can be trusted" with new ones: "This feels different. I can breathe here."

3. Trust Is Built When Words and Actions Align

Trust isn't just about what people say—it's about whether their actions match their words. This includes:

- Showing up when they say they will
- Following through on commitments
- Owning mistakes without deflection
- Expressing emotion in ways that feel congruent, not performative

When words and actions align, the body relaxes. When they don't, the body tenses—and that tension is a clue.

Trusting yourself also requires alignment:

- Do you keep the promises you make to yourself?
- Do you respect your own boundaries?
- Do you pause before self-abandoning for connection?

The more you trust your own internal signals, the less you depend on others to define what is safe.

4. Trust Can Be Repaired—But It Requires Accountability

In any relationship, trust will be strained at times. But it can be restored through:

- Acknowledging harm without defensiveness
- Expressing impact, not just intention
- Asking what's needed for repair—and then following through
- Creating a consistent pattern of behavior that invites safety

You don't have to be perfect to be trusted. But you do have to be *present, accountable, and consistent*.

When both people in a relationship commit to this slow, steady building of trust, intimacy begins to deepen naturally. Vulnerability becomes less scary. Communication becomes more honest. And presence becomes more stable.

But trust can't grow in chaos. It needs something more: **emotional availability**—the capacity to remain open and attuned over time.

The Role of Consistency and Emotional Availability
Emotional availability is not about being emotionally "on" all the time. It's about being *accessible, responsive, and engaged* enough to support connection. For attachment healing, this is the bedrock of intimacy. Without it, even the most open-hearted person will feel alone.

Many people believe they are emotionally available—but availability is not a trait; it's a practice. It looks like:

- Checking in regularly—not just when there's a problem
- Being able to sit with someone else's emotion without needing to fix or flee
- Offering empathy instead of defensiveness
- Remaining open even when conversations are difficult
- Being willing to talk about relational dynamics, not just logistics

In attachment terms, emotional availability means staying **attuned**. It means noticing when someone shifts, asks for closeness, or begins to withdraw—and responding not with fear or control, but with curiosity and presence.

For anxiously attached individuals, emotional availability often becomes *hyperavailability*. They may overextend, over-disclose, or become fused with their partner's emotional state. They're always "on," not because they feel secure, but because they fear disconnection.

For avoidantly attached individuals, emotional availability often feels threatening. They may withdraw, intellectualize, or minimize their own feelings to avoid discomfort. This creates a pattern where they are physically present but emotionally absent.

To cultivate *healthy* emotional availability:

- **Start with your own emotional world**: Are you aware of your feelings? Do you allow yourself to feel them? Can you soothe yourself without shutting down?
- **Develop emotional vocabulary**: Move beyond "I'm fine" or "I'm stressed." Learn to name primary emotions—hurt, shame, joy, fear, hope.
- **Make time for emotional check-ins**: With yourself and others. Ask, "What's happening in me right now?" and "What's happening between us?"
- **Practice emotional presence** without problem-solving: Sit with someone's sadness. Let it be. Offer connection, not correction.

Consistency is what transforms these practices from gestures into trust-building rituals.

It's not about dramatic declarations or constant affirmation. It's about:

- Showing up when it matters
- Staying steady when things get tough
- Being emotionally honest, even when it's vulnerable
- Creating a relational rhythm that says, *"You can count on me."*

And that rhythm is what heals. Because the nervous system doesn't just want love—it wants *predictable*, *safe*, *reliable* love. Love that doesn't punish emotion. Love that makes space for both independence and connection. Love that allows you to relax.

This kind of love begins inside. And from there, it extends outward—not as performance, but as presence. Not as an obligation, but as an offering.

You begin to say, without fear: *"I'm here. I can stay. And I can let you stay too."*

PART V: SUSTAINABLE GROWTH AND LASTING CONNECTIONS

Chapter 13: Becoming Secure — Shifting from Pattern to Choice

What Earned Secure Attachment Looks Like

Secure attachment is not perfection. It's not the absence of triggers, fear, or need. Instead, it is the ability to navigate life and relationships with a grounded sense of *inner stability*. When security is earned—not inherited—it is the result of deep inner work, consistent self-reflection, and repeated corrective experiences.

People with secure attachment do not always feel confident. They feel uncertainty, disappointment, anger, and fear. The difference is that they trust their ability to respond *instead of react*. They know their emotions will not destroy them. They know closeness doesn't require self-erasure, and distance doesn't mean rejection. They are anchored in themselves, and from that place, they can extend genuine connection.

Here's what **earned secure attachment** looks like in practice:

1. Emotional Responsiveness Without Reactivity

You don't deny your emotions, but you don't get swallowed by them either. When hurt, you acknowledge the feeling and respond thoughtfully. When triggered, you pause before acting. You allow space for your nervous system to regulate before engaging from fear.

2. Honest, Boundaried Communication

You express your needs clearly, without guilt or apology. You respect your limits—and those of others. You don't overshare to gain closeness or stay silent to avoid discomfort. Your words carry self-respect, and your tone invites trust.

3. Mutuality and Interdependence

You no longer confuse independence with avoidance or closeness with codependency. You value reciprocal relationships where both people matter. You can ask for support without shame, and offer support without resentment.

4. Stability in the Face of Uncertainty

You're able to tolerate the discomfort of relational ambiguity without spiraling. A delayed text or a tough conversation no longer feels catastrophic. You can hold emotional complexity—your own and others'—without rushing to fix or flee.

5. Curiosity Over Assumption

Rather than interpreting behavior through the lens of old wounds, you inquire. You ask questions instead of making accusations. You stay open instead of shutting down.

6. Presence in Conflict and Repair

You no longer avoid conflict out of fear or escalate it out of panic. You're willing to rupture and repair. You take responsibility for your part. You stay engaged even when it's uncomfortable.

7. Deep Self-Trust

At the core of secure attachment is this truth: *You trust yourself to handle what arises.* This doesn't mean you never struggle—it means you don't abandon yourself in the struggle. You stay. You support. You soothe. And you choose aligned action.

Earned secure attachment is not a destination. It's a living process—a relationship with yourself that becomes the foundation for every other relationship in your life.

And that process only becomes sustainable when you stop living from pattern and start living from *choice*.

Choosing Differently in Love and Conflict
Becoming securely attached doesn't mean you'll never be triggered again. It means that when you are, you recognize it. You pause. You respond with intention, not compulsion. You choose differently.

This is the fundamental shift from **pattern** to **choice**.

Patterns Are Predictable but Unconscious
Attachment patterns are automatic. They are survival responses developed to protect you from emotional pain. They operate beneath awareness and often feel like the truth. For example:

- "They didn't reply. I must have done something wrong."

- "If I say what I need, they'll leave."
- "I feel overwhelmed—I need to pull away now."
- "If I forgive them, I'm weak."

These thoughts trigger behaviors—texting rapidly, people-pleasing, stonewalling, cutting off—that keep the cycle alive. You feel temporarily safe but ultimately disconnected, ashamed, or misunderstood.

Choice Is Conscious, Grounded, and Liberating
When you begin to heal, you gain space between stimulus and response. You still feel the urge to react—but you pause. You ask:

- "What's really happening right now?"
- "What's my intention here—connection or protection?"
- "Is this response aligned with who I am becoming?"
- "Can I sit with this discomfort a little longer before acting?"

That pause is power. It allows you to:

- Express needs without escalating
- Say no without guilt
- Stay present when you want to disappear
- Validate your feelings without outsourcing them
- Choose partners, friends, and environments that match your healed self

In Love: Choosing Alignment Over Attachment Anxiety
You begin to choose people who feel emotionally safe—not just exciting. You no longer chase those who

invalidate you or feel responsible for managing someone else's dysregulation. You prioritize consistency, mutual respect, and healthy reciprocity.

You can tolerate a partner needing space without losing your center. You don't confuse drama with passion or silence with punishment. You don't need constant reassurance to know you're loved.

In Conflict: Choosing Repair Over Retaliation
When hurt, you pause instead of lashing out or collapsing. You communicate from grounded emotion—not from survival instinct. You don't make your partner responsible for fixing you, but you do invite connection.

You stop replaying the same old arguments. Instead, you co-create new scripts. You ask, "How can we stay connected even when we disagree?"

This shift from pattern to choice doesn't mean you don't feel. It means you *respond in service of relationship, not reaction*.

Each time you do, you reinforce a new reality: *I can handle this. I can stay connected to myself and others. I am safe to love.*

And over time, you start to notice something extraordinary: your old pain no longer runs the show. You're not perfect—but you're present. You're not invulnerable—but you're brave.

You've healed enough to choose again.

Identifying When You've Healed (And What's Next)
Healing from attachment wounds isn't always a lightning-bolt moment. It's more like waking up one day and realizing you didn't overreact to something that used to unravel you. It's noticing you felt triggered—but didn't text. It's hearing "no" without hearing "you're unlovable."

So how do you know when you've reached a state of *earned secure attachment*? What are the signs that you're living from a place of wholeness—not wound?

Here are subtle but powerful indicators:

1. Emotional Regulation Comes More Easily

You still feel—but you don't feel powerless. You experience fear, sadness, frustration—but you trust those feelings will pass. You don't make urgent decisions in the middle of a spiral. You pause, you ground, you choose.

2. Boundaries Are Clear and Sustainable

You say yes when it feels aligned and no when it doesn't. You don't explain yourself excessively or collapse under guilt. You respect others' limits and your own. You stop over-functioning to avoid discomfort.

3. You Value Mutual, Not Transactional, Relationships

You no longer stay in one-sided dynamics. You seek emotional availability, not just chemistry. You know the difference between someone who activates your nervous system and someone who nourishes it.

4. You Repair, Not Repeat

Old conflicts don't keep resurfacing. You take ownership. You forgive when ready. You listen more than you defend. You communicate with curiosity. You choose connection over control.

5. You Feel Safe in Solitude

Being alone no longer feels like abandonment. You know your own company. You enjoy your own thoughts. You don't need constant connection to feel whole. And you don't confuse independence with isolation.

6. You Feel Compassion for the Old You

You stop judging your past self for their patterns. You feel tenderness for the anxious you who texted ten times. For the avoidant you who shut down mid-conversation. For those of you who didn't know how to stay present. They were surviving. Now, you're *living*.

7. You Look Ahead With Intention

Healing brings vision. You begin to ask: *What kind of relationships do I want to cultivate? How do I want to love? What legacy of emotional safety do I want to leave behind?*

You stop surviving love—and start designing it.

What's next?
What comes after healing is not a finish line—but a *new way of relating*. A life where you:

- Love from freedom, not fear
- Communicate with clarity, not compulsion
- Stay open even when it's hard
- Choose people who choose you—not because you need them to, but because you *want* them to

And when new challenges arise—and they will—you no longer regress. You *return*. You return to the tools. The awareness. The breath. The self-trust.

You return to *you*.

This is the reward of the work: not immunity from pain, but the unshakable belief that no matter what happens—you will not abandon yourself again.

You've earned your security.

You've become the safe space you once longed for.

And from here, everything changes.

Chapter 14: Navigating Attachment in Friendships and Families

Not Just Romantic: Attachment Shows Up Everywhere

Attachment dynamics are often discussed in the context of romantic relationships—but they don't begin or end there. In truth, the roots of your attachment system are embedded in the earliest relationships: with parents, caregivers, and close family members. And as you grow, those patterns continue to echo—not only in partnerships, but also in friendships, sibling bonds, and even work or spiritual communities.

The nervous system doesn't categorize love. It doesn't distinguish between types of intimacy. It simply reacts to closeness, vulnerability, and perceived threat. Whether you're with a partner, a friend, a sibling, or a parent, your attachment history informs how you show up—how you connect, how you protect, how you repair.

This is why healing work must extend beyond dating and romance. You can be securely attached to a partner but still feel defensive around your mother. You may express needs easily with friends but freeze in emotional conversations with siblings. Each relationship touches a different part of your attachment landscape.

Here's how attachment patterns tend to show up in **non-romantic contexts**:

In Friendships:

- **Anxiously attached individuals** may become overly invested or fear being left out. They might

over-give, suppress their needs, or feel devastated by perceived distance.
- **Avoidantly attached individuals** might keep friendships surface-level, avoid emotional depth, or withdraw when vulnerability arises.
- **Disorganized attachment** may show up as alternating between intense closeness and sudden distance, often driven by mistrust or fear of betrayal.

In Family Systems:

- **Old roles** (the fixer, the black sheep, the peacekeeper) are often unconsciously reenacted.
- Emotional triggers are stronger, because they were often formed in the same environment.
- Attempts at boundary-setting can be met with confusion, guilt, or backlash, especially in enmeshed or rigid families.

Friendships and family dynamics offer powerful opportunities for growth because they reflect different dimensions of your relational identity. You may find your voice in friendships before you find it at home. Or you may begin healing family wounds only after learning how safety feels in chosen relationships.

The key to navigating these dynamics is recognizing that **your attachment style is a map, not a destiny**. Just because you learned to hide, cling, or shut down in one environment doesn't mean you're doomed to repeat it forever. With awareness, choice, and care, you can create new ways of relating—even with those who've known you the longest.

But for that to happen, you often need to address the most challenging terrain of all: family.

Repairing with Parents, Siblings, and Adult Children

Family relationships carry deep emotional charge. They are the original site of your attachment learning—and often the most resistant to change. Healing here is not about rewriting history, but about rewriting your role within it.

When you start to grow, family systems often resist. You stop people-pleasing, and someone accuses you of being selfish. You set a boundary, and suddenly you're "too sensitive." You try to express your truth, and you're met with silence or emotional shutdown.

This resistance isn't always malicious. In many cases, it's rooted in fear—fear that your change will disrupt the fragile balance the family has maintained, even if it's been dysfunctional. But just because your healing makes others uncomfortable doesn't mean it's wrong.

Here's how to navigate family repair thoughtfully and intentionally:

1. Clarify Your Intention Before You Engage

Ask yourself:

- What do I hope will come from this conversation or reconnection?
- Am I seeking validation, or am I offering perspective?

- Do I want to rebuild, set boundaries, or simply be heard?

Having a clear goal helps you stay grounded and reduces the risk of falling into old patterns or power struggles.

2. Accept That Some Family Members May Never Change

This is one of the hardest truths in attachment work: not everyone will evolve with you. Some parents will never take accountability. Some siblings will stay emotionally unavailable. Some relatives will choose denial over reflection.

But healing doesn't require their participation. It requires your *clarity, boundaries, and compassion*. You can forgive without condoning. You can love from a distance. You can grieve what they cannot offer—and still find peace.

3. Practice Low-Expectation Conversations

Instead of jumping into deep emotional confrontation, start with small, honest moments:

- "That comment hurt me. I want you to know how it landed."
- "I've been working on some patterns from childhood, and I've realized how they affected our dynamic."
- "I want a more honest relationship, and I'm learning how to show up differently."

Not every conversation will lead to breakthrough—but each one is a step toward integrity.

4. Repair Through Boundaries, Not Just Words

Sometimes the most healing act is not an apology—but a change in behavior. You can't force others to respect your boundaries, but you can model them consistently:

- "I'm not available for late-night calls anymore."
- "I can't discuss this topic if it becomes disrespectful."
- "If the conversation turns aggressive, I'll step away and revisit later."

Healthy families adapt. Dysfunctional ones resist. Your role is not to convince them—but to stay aligned with what is emotionally healthy for you.

5. For Adult Children and Parenting Repair: Lead with Vulnerability

If you're repairing with your own adult children, begin with ownership, not defensiveness:

- "Looking back, I see ways I hurt you—even without meaning to."
- "I wasn't always emotionally present, and I regret that."
- "I want to keep learning how to love you better. Will you help me understand your experience?"

These conversations require humility and patience. But they also open doors. They signal safety. They invite re-connection—not through guilt, but through authenticity.

Repairing with family is not about rewriting the past. It's about creating a new future—one where you are no longer a prisoner of your childhood role, but the author of your adult presence.

And sometimes, creating that future means making the hardest decision of all: choosing *when* to engage, *when* to step back, and *when* to forgive.

When to Engage, Disengage, or Forgive

Not every relationship should be salvaged. Not every bond must be maintained. Healing sometimes means staying—but it also sometimes means walking away with clarity and love. Learning *when* to engage, disengage, or forgive is part of becoming securely attached—because it means you are no longer driven by guilt, fear, or obligation.

Here's how to discern your next step in challenging relational dynamics:

1. Engage When There Is Mutual Openness and Safety

Engagement requires *emotional safety*—even if the relationship is imperfect. If the other person:

- Shows willingness to reflect
- Respects your boundaries (even if imperfectly)
- Apologizes when they cause harm
- Demonstrates care in action, not just words

Then the relationship has the potential to evolve. Rebuild slowly. Stay curious. Create new patterns together.

2. Disengage When the Pattern Is Consistently Harmful

If a relationship consistently causes harm, and repair is not possible or welcome, it may be time to step away. This does not require drama or hostility. Disengagement can be quiet, clear, and compassionate.

Signs it may be time to disengage:

- You feel chronically anxious, drained, or disrespected
- Your boundaries are repeatedly violated
- Conversations are weaponized against you
- You are expected to carry the emotional burden without reciprocity

Disengagement is not abandonment—it is self-protection. It is choosing emotional health over obligation. It is releasing yourself from dynamics that keep you small, reactive, or stuck.

3. Forgive When It Liberates You—Not When It Silences You

Forgiveness is a personal process. It does not mean excusing behavior or inviting someone back into your life. It means releasing *yourself* from the grip of resentment, revenge, or unprocessed grief.

You forgive when:

- You're ready to free your energy
- You want to stop re-enacting the past
- You've honored your pain and are ready to set it down

Forgiveness is not always verbal. It doesn't require reconciliation. It is an internal letting go that creates room for peace.

You can forgive someone and still hold boundaries.
You can love someone and still choose distance.
You can grieve a relationship and still feel whole.

This is what attachment healing looks like in the real world—not just in theory, but in family gatherings, phone calls, holidays, group chats, and long silences. It is the quiet, courageous decision to choose *your truth*—and to relate from a place of *presence, not pattern.*

When you engage, disengage, or forgive with awareness, you become the secure presence your family system never had. You break cycles. You repair within. And you model a new way forward for everyone around you—without forcing them to follow.

Chapter 15: Future Relationships Built on Emotional Integrity

Red Flags vs. Growth Opportunities in New Relationships

As you heal from insecure attachment and begin relating from a place of earned security, the way you perceive relationships fundamentally changes. What once seemed exciting may now feel dysregulating. What once went unnoticed may now set off a quiet alarm. You're no longer desperate to attach—you're discerning. You're not searching for someone to complete you—you're seeking someone who complements your wholeness.

But discernment doesn't mean closing off. It means learning how to differentiate between patterns you must protect yourself from and opportunities where you—and the other person—can grow.

Let's begin with **red flags**—not as scary signs to panic over, but as *invitations to pause and assess*. A red flag is any consistent behavior, communication style, or emotional pattern that compromises your sense of safety, clarity, or self-respect. They don't always mean "walk away immediately," but they do mean "pay attention."

Common Red Flags in Early Relationships:

- *Inconsistency*: frequent changes in behavior, affection, or communication without explanation
- *Defensiveness*: inability to hear feedback, constant justification, or attacking when challenged

- *Lack of accountability*: blaming others, avoiding repair, or rewriting past events
- *Emotional unavailability*: dismissing feelings, avoiding depth, or withholding vulnerability
- *Love bombing*: intense, premature declarations of affection that lack relational foundation
- *Boundary disrespect*: ignoring or pushing past your stated limits—physically, emotionally, or verbally

When you encounter these signs, check in with yourself:

- *Do I feel grounded in this connection—or anxious, confused, or drained?*
- *Am I making excuses for behavior that doesn't sit well with me?*
- *Do I feel safe expressing my needs? Are they met with respect?*

If the answer is no, it doesn't mean the person is bad. It means the *dynamic* may be misaligned with your healing. You can communicate concerns—but you're not obligated to stay in environments that consistently ignore or erode your emotional safety.

Now contrast this with **growth opportunities**—moments in a new relationship where imperfection shows up, but so does willingness, presence, and openness to evolve.

Signs of Growth Potential:

- The other person expresses vulnerability and invites yours in return

- Conflict, when it arises, leads to repair—not rupture
- They respect your boundaries, even if they don't fully understand them yet
- You both speak and listen from a place of emotional honesty
- You feel more regulated with them than without them
- There is space for individuality and togetherness—without pressure

In early secure relationships, you may not feel fireworks. You may feel *calm*. That calm is not boredom—it's safe. It's the absence of chaos. It's the space where real connection can grow.

Learn to choose relational **alignment** over emotional intensity. Choose character over charisma. Choose someone whose actions match their words—especially when things aren't easy.

When you do, you stop chasing red flags disguised as chemistry. You begin building relationships where growth, not wounding, becomes the foundation.

Maintaining Secure Attachment in Long-Term Love
Healing isn't something you do *before* a relationship—it's something you *continue* doing *within* one. While singlehood may provide the clarity to recognize patterns, it is long-term relationships that reveal your deepest emotional edges. The presence of sustained love will surface anything that blocks your ability to fully receive it.

That's why earned secure attachment isn't just about *finding* the right person. It's about *becoming* the kind of person who can stay emotionally present, regulated, and open through the inevitable ebbs and flows of long-term connection.

Here's how secure attachment is maintained in daily relational life:

1. Continue Practicing Self-Regulation

Your nervous system is your responsibility. No matter how loving your partner is, they cannot consistently regulate you. When conflict arises, secure couples:

- Take space when needed—but with communication
- Reconnect after rupture—not just coexist in silence
- Soothe themselves rather than demand soothing as proof of love

When you feel yourself reverting to old patterns—stonewalling, pleasing, over-apologizing—pause. Breathe. Return to yourself. Then re-engage from a more grounded place.

2. Use Conflict as a Catalyst for Intimacy

Insecure attachment sees conflict as danger. Secure attachment sees it as *data*. Conflict reveals unmet needs, misalignments, and opportunities for deeper understanding.

Secure partners:

- Name emotions without blame
- Acknowledge hurt without shame
- Take responsibility without collapsing
- Listen with the intent to understand, not just respond

You don't have to "win" arguments. You have to stay connected *through* them.

3. Keep Reaffirming Boundaries and Needs

Needs and boundaries evolve. What worked a year ago may not work now. Check in with your partner regularly:

- "Is there anything you need more or less of from me?"
- "Have any of our routines stopped working for you?"
- "Is there something we've been avoiding that we should revisit?"

These small conversations prevent silent resentment and reinforce emotional safety.

4. Prioritize Emotional Rituals

Long-term love can become logistical—about bills, chores, and schedules. Make space for connection:

- Daily check-ins: "How are you feeling today?"
- Weekly touchpoints: "How are we doing emotionally?"
- Shared mindfulness, cuddling, eye contact, and laughter

These rituals don't take much time—but they deepen intimacy and anchor your attachment.

5. Grow Together, Not Just Alongside Each Other

Attachment security is nourished by **shared evolution**. Support each other's personal development. Celebrate emotional breakthroughs. Stay curious about who the other is becoming.

Ask:

- "What's something you've been learning about yourself lately?"
- "Is there a way I can support your growth better?"
- "What's something you're proud of in how you've been showing up?"

Love, when held with care, becomes a mirror—not of who you were, but of who you are becoming.

Secure couples don't avoid pain. They learn to stay together in it. Not perfectly—but with presence. With practice. With deep trust in the connection they are building every day.

Living Authentically and Loving From Wholeness

In the end, attachment healing leads to something far greater than better relationships—it leads to *alignment with your truest self*. You begin living—not as the version of you shaped by fear, scarcity, or conditioning—but as the person who feels safe in their own presence. Who knows what they want. Who no longer shrinks or performs to be loved.

To love from *wholeness* means:

- You are not looking for someone to complete you—but to connect with you
- You do not abandon yourself to maintain closeness
- You show up with truth, even if it risks discomfort
- You love generously, but not at your own expense
- You choose relationships that honor who you are—not who you had to be

Living authentically starts with **self-ownership**. You stop blaming your past. You stop waiting for someone to rescue you. You meet yourself fully—with compassion and clarity. And from that place, you create a life that matches your inner alignment.

Here's how to embody that daily:

1. Let Your Values Lead

Decide how you want to show up—in love, work, friendship, and solitude. Let integrity guide your choices. Say:

- "This relationship aligns with my value of emotional honesty."
- "This job supports my need for balance."
- "This friendship brings out the version of me I love most."

When your external world reflects your internal truth, peace follows.

2. Surround Yourself with Secure People

You don't have to fix others to feel worthy. You don't have to prove yourself to earn care. Seek out people who:

- Respect your emotions without trying to change them
- Celebrate your boundaries, not challenge them
- Take responsibility when they cause harm
- Offer presence, not perfection

Let your nervous system relax in good company. Let love feel like rest, not labor.

3. Be Willing to Walk Alone if It Protects Your Wholeness

Some seasons require solitude. Not because you're unlovable—but because you're *refining your self-connection*. Being alone while securely attached is not emptiness—it's empowerment. It's the ability to say: *I will not abandon myself for belonging.*

When you live from wholeness, loneliness loses its grip. You become a full person—not a half waiting for another.

4. Keep Healing Forward

Even after years of work, you'll still have moments of doubt. You'll still get triggered. But now, you know how to pause. How to return. How to choose again. Healing is not a finish line. It is a practice. A devotion. A way of living with yourself.

The reward is not a perfect relationship. It's a *wholehearted one*. One where you don't have to edit your truth to be loved. One where you speak, and your voice doesn't tremble. One where you are not tolerated—you are *met*.

This is the life that secure attachment offers. Not because someone gave it to you. But because you *became it*.

As you close this book, know this:
You are already worthy of the love you seek.
You are already whole, even if still healing.
You are not your patterns—you are your presence.
You are safe to love.
And you are safe to be loved.

Made in the USA
Columbia, SC
11 July 2025